OP 7⁵⁰

THE PROGRESS OF SOCIETY IN EUROPE

CLASSIC EUROPEAN HISTORIANS

A SERIES EDITED BY LEONARD KRIEGER

William Robertson

THE PROGRESS
OF SOCIETY IN EUROPE

*A Historical Outline
from the Subversion of the Roman Empire
to the Beginning of the Sixteenth Century*

Edited and with an Introduction

by Felix Gilbert

THE UNIVERSITY OF CHICAGO PRESS
CHICAGO & LONDON

THE UNIVERSITY OF CHICAGO PRESS, CHICAGO 60637
THE UNIVERSITY OF CHICAGO PRESS, LTD., LONDON

© 1972 by The University of Chicago
All rights reserved
Published 1972
Printed in the United States of America

International Standard Book Number: 0–226–72133–7 (clothbound)
Library of Congress Catalog Card Number: 75–190283

Contents

Series Editor's Preface

THE introductory volume of William Robertson's *History of the Reign of Charles V* (1769), reedited herewith by Felix Gilbert, is the Enlightenment's entry in the Classic European Historians. Like the series as a whole, it is reproduced to serve both historical and historiographical purposes—that is, to present an illuminated piece of our past and to demonstrate the point of view of the historians who have illuminated it—and it serves this joint purpose with surprising equipoise, considering its mid-eighteenth-century vintage. That Robertson would be historiographically interesting was indeed to be expected, since Enlightenment historians have ever provoked enthusiastic response, whether of attack or rehabilitation. But it was not to be expected that his work would retain historical value for what it shows of the past. Not only do historians in general assume a law of progress in scholarship which tends automatically to equate old history with superseded history, but a particular survey by an Enlightenment historian of Europe's development through the middle ages—such as this volume of Robertson is—would seem to be particularly negligible as history, worthy of attention at most as a matter of curiosity, amusement, or self-congratulatory condescension.

Yet the revaluation of Robertson the historian which Professor Gilbert achieves in his admirably lucid introduction is such as to revalidate the history as well. The tendency of recent scholarship to rescue the historiography of the Enlightenment from its nineteenth-century opprobium has applied rather to the approach than the results of eighteenth-century historians, but Professor Gilbert's reassessment goes beyond this now familiar tendency and shows in Robertson a historian whose hidden complexity not only reflected an unsuspected sophistication in approach but also produced an unappreciated authenticity in result. For Robertson is now shown to have combined, in more equivalent proportion than any of his celebrated contemporaries, the two main accomplishments of eighteenth-century historiography, which usually followed separate paths with only sporadic intersection. The first was a new version of universal history which conceived universality vertically and considered it to be the whole of human culture within a definite time-span rather than the traditional horizontal narrative of world history through the sundry ecclesiastico-political ages since the Creation. The second was the advanced technique of validating and collecting historical sources, religious and legal particularly, which, initiated during the previous century, inspired the flourishing enterprise of processing ecclesiastical and constitutional origins so prominently associated with the Maurists in France, Muratori in Italy, and Leibniz in Germany. Professor Gilbert shows just how Robertson wove the two strands together, thereby attaining an especially representative status in respect to Enlightenment historiography and an especially respected status for his general history.

The point is not, of course, that Robertson's medieval context of modern Europe is comparable to the results emerging from the more specialized and socialized research of medievalists in our own century. The point is rather that in Robertson's hands the distinctive values of Enlightenment historiography contributed to his history dimensions that at once were inimitable by nineteenth-century historians and again relevant to us of the twentieth-century. Two such dimensions may be pointed out here as particularly outstanding guide-posts in Robertson to revalidated Enlightenment history.

First, his survey of European "progress" in the middle ages, which he so often condemned, constructively applied to actual history the discrepancy between causes and effects which was a signal contribution of the Enlightenment to the understanding of human affairs and which has once again become an operational conviction in our own day. The perception began with Mandeville's social transmutation of private vices into public virtues and culminated in Kant's and Hegel's famous references to reason's hypothetical or cunning alchemization of self-regarding passions into the bonds of community as a necessary conclusion from the Enlightenment's secularized approach to universal history. In Robertson's conscientious acknowledgment of the beneficial effects attributable to malevolent causes—most notably the modernizing result of the atrocious Crusades, the constitutional influence of the feuding nobility, and the unifying effect of authoritarian monarchy—we can see this principle at work in Enlightenment historiography, with all the loosening and liberating implications which have become explicit in our own disjointed attitude toward the historical process. And in Robertson's blend of the three divergent canons which lay behind this precocious recognition of the unpredictable in history—that is, his blend of critical judgment upon medieval historical action, of teleological direction in interpreting its results for the modern age, and of fidelity to his historical sources independently of his moral standards and his progressive interests—we can see the origins of the irreducible plurality of principles which constitutes the modern historical sense and somehow produces what we call satisfactory history. His was, moreover, a representative rather than an individual performance. The Enlightenment's pride in its own rationality as the emergent measure of universal history and its simultaneous fascination with the spatially, temporally, and culturally exotic were equally explicit in Robertson, and the accessibility of Europe's Middle Ages to both attitudes in his treatment goes far to explain the surprising extent of the eighteenth-century concern with medieval history which has been uncovered by recent scholarship.

The other obvious dimension of lasting interest in Robertson's portrait of the European prelude to modernity is its readability—

an essential quality of historical writing in the Enlightenment, reflecting its view of history as a species of literature subject to the general standards of style, composition, and entertainment. These standards make Robertson's historical description of medieval institutions, like the rise of feudalism and comparative constitutions, fit for the consumption of a larger audience than the more recent and more professional textbooks and monographs on such subjects have managed to attract, but the literary feature of Enlightenment historiography here exemplified has a meaning that goes beyond its appeal to the uncoerced reader. Professor Gilbert's shrewd selection of samples from Robertson's voluminous "proofs and illustrations" uncovers the artfully camouflaged depths of detailed information from which this Enlightenment historian distilled the smooth, graceful, and coherent flow of his main text. Surely there is a model here for all of us—professional and amateur alike—who try our hand at writing history.

LEONARD KRIEGER

Editor's Introduction

OF the three eminent historical writers produced by the British Enlightenment—Edward Gibbon, David Hume, and William Robertson—Robertson is the least known. Paradoxically enough, what might be regarded as his most outstanding virtue is a reason for this neglect: His historical writings approach the scholarly standards which were to be developed in the nineteenth century and are judged according to them. The histories of Gibbon and Hume, on the other hand, are studied for the light which they throw on the minds of their authors, and as expressions and reflections of the thought of the Enlightenment; whether their histories are factually correct is considered to be of limited interest. Nevertheless, Robertson's histories should not be viewed as works that once were famous and can now be disregarded. They remain interesting from two points of view. Like Gibbon's and Hume's writings, they are significant expressions of the mind of the Enlightenment; moreover, they demonstrate an early stage in the development of the concepts and methods of modern historical research. Robertson's most famous work, his "View of the Progress of Society in Europe," with which he opened his *History of the Reign of the Emperor Charles V*, deserves to be counted among the classics of European historical writing.

I

The pleasantly old-fashioned "Life of Dr. Robertson," which prefaces an early edition of Robertson's collected works, begins with the statement: "If the laws of equity are to be observed in the republic of learning no man possesses a greater claim than an historian to have his life carefully recorded. He who has devoted his labor and ingenuity to the task of describing the exploits of others deserves that his own actions should not be forgotten by the many readers whom he has studied to please and enlighten." The idea that the life of every historian deserves to be immortalized in a biography is flattering to the practitioners of the historical profession, but if it can be justified at all it can hardly be justified by the life of William Robertson. Although his life was active and influential, it was devoid of dramatic events.

With the exception of a few brief vacation trips to London, Robertson's life and career evolved in Edinburgh and its surroundings. He was born in 1721 in a small place in Midlothian where his father was a minister. But in 1733 his father was called to Edinburgh, and young Robertson entered the university. It was not unusual at this time for boys who had received a good grounding in the classics to begin their university studies at an early age. After leaving the university, Robertson was for fifteen years minister at Gladsmuir in East Lothian, not more than twenty miles from Edinburgh. During these years he was able to keep up his contacts in the Scotch capital. He returned to Edinburgh in 1758, first as minister at Lady Yester's Chapel, then at the Old Greyfriars Church. But although he continued in these ecclesiastical duties until his death in 1793, he also filled other positions which were of greater importance and on which he concentrated most of his energies. In 1762 he became Principal of the University of Edinburgh and his administration contributed greatly to the growth of the university. Outstanding men were added to the faculty; much attention was given to the improvement of the medical school; and arrangements were made for the construction of larger, more adequate buildings. From 1763 to 1780 Robertson was also Moderator of the General Assembly of the Church of Scotland. His attitude in church affairs was mildly progressive and conciliatory. He was instrumental in settling the conflict between those who defended the patronage owners' right to present the minister of the church and those who stressed the paramount importance of the "call" by the members of the parish. The conflict was solved by reducing the "call" of the parish members to "concurrence" to take place after presentation of the minister by the patron. When Robertson was appointed Principal and elected Moderator, he was already a man of literary fame. In 1759 his *History of Scotland* had appeared and had established him as a leader in the intellectual world of Edinburgh.

In these years literary eminence in Scotland also meant possession of a European reputation. This was the time of the Scottish Renaissance, the rise and triumph of which coincided with Robertson's active years. There is an amusing example of the change in the intellectual climate of Edinburgh which, under the influence of the Enlightenment, took place during Robertson's lifetime. In 1751 Robertson, intervening for the first time in the General Assembly of the church, spoke in defense of some ministers who had been to the theater to see the first production of John Home's *Douglas*. Robertson made a strong impression because he could not only say that he had been innocent of this crime but also that he never had and never would enter within the walls of a playhouse. Twenty-seven years later, in 1784, Sara Siddons was in Edinburgh, and her performances coincided with the meeting of the General Assembly: "The county clergy went in crowds to see her and no notice was taken of it by the Assembly. Nay, the Assembly itself by vote postponed a great cause to a day on which she was not to play in case the Assembly house should have been thin in the afternoon."

Robertson was not only an observer but an active promoter of these intellectual changes. In 1754 he had been one of the founders of the "Select Society" which included "all the individuals in Edinburgh and the neighborhood who were much distinguished by genius or by literary attainments." Members of this society from its beginnings were David Hume, Adam Smith, Adam Ferguson, Alexander Carlyle, Lord Kames, and John Home. This was the circle with which Robertson remained associated throughout his life. However, memoirs from this group leave the impression that there was some distance between Robertson and the other Scotch literati. Robertson seems to have been very conscious of the importance and dignity which his high administrative positions gave him. He was pompous and liked to shine. One of his contemporaries asserted that he never "saw him patiently bear anybody else's showing off but Dr. Johnson and Garrick." In Robertson the views of a man of the Enlightenment were combined with a strong feeling for the importance of institutions and hierarchy, and this combination of a modern and a traditional element—of Enlightenment thought and university learning—also constitutes the peculiar and distinctive character of his historical work.

II

The first impression which "A View of the Progress of Society in Europe" gives to the reader is that it was written by a man who belonged to the school of the philosophes. Robertson refers to Ferguson and Hume, to Montesquieu, Mably, and Voltaire. The basic assumptions of the work—even more than these appeals to the authority of prominent philosophes—show the impact of Enlightenment thought. Robertson regarded himself as living in "enlightened times"; the significant feature of this era was the adoption of reason as a guide in human behavior. In contrast to the eighteenth century, the Middle Ages, in which the light of reason had only dimly flickered, were for Robertson "dark ages." They abounded in "deeds of cruelty, perfidy and revenge so wild and enormous as almost to exceed belief"; the religion which the people of the Middle Ages practiced was only nominally Christian; actually it was pure superstition. Belief in the supreme value of reason limited Robertson's historical understanding; he denied all historical significance to those medieval enterprises which were inspired by religion: the Crusades were for him "a singular monument of human folly," and the subjection of litigation to a "judgment by God," which was a first step towards the replacement of blood revenge by regular legal proceedings, appeared to Robertson "among all the whimsical and absurd institutions which owe their existence to the weaknesses of human reason . . . the most extravagant and preposterous."

Robertson's explanation for the progress from the "barbarism" of the Middle Ages to the "refinement" of his own time was not different from that of the other philosophes. The crucial fact was "commerce," which "softens and polishes the manners of men," creates a community among nations, and brings them closer together so that old prejudices and animosities disappear. Commerce makes men interested in the maintenance of security and tranquillity, and appreciative of the benefits of peace. Robertson saw a relation between wealth on one side and laws, subordination, and polished manners on the other. Although ostentation and luxury were dangers inherent in the accumulation of wealth, such dangers appeared to Robertson minor in comparison to the advantages which he believed accrued from the impact of wealth on the formation of an ordered society.

Robertson had no less confidence in the possibilities and opportunities of the age of reason in which he lived than did other philosophes. However, he was not a utopian who believed that history had reached a final stage, that war and politics were ending, and that a global society without frontiers enjoying permanent peace was near to being established. Robertson's views about the influence of reason on foreign policy did not go beyond maintaining that in his age "the adventurous exploits of chivalry" had been replaced by "the well-regulated operations of sound policy." "Sound policy" was for Robertson identical with a rational policy based on the calculable permanent interests of states. Robertson wrote in his *History of Scotland* that "the great secret of modern politics" was the "balance of power," and he reiterated this idea in similar terms in the *History of the Reign of Charles V*, where he spoke of "that great secret in modern policy, the preservation of a proper distribution of power." Recognition of the principle of balance of power appeared to Robertson to be one of the great attainments of modern times which had purged irrational, violent, cruel elements from politics. The "modern politician" had become aware that every change which increased the strength of one state would have an impact on the position of any other, even geographically remote and not immediately involved. Rulers had learned that their independence was tied up with the fate of every other state. They carefully observed every move on the political chessboard and had become cautious in their plans and actions. All the European states were members of one and the same system.

The notion of balance was also central for Robertson's views on the internal organization of the European states. The feudal government of the Middle Ages was weak because "the monarchical and aristocratical parts of the constitution, having no intermediate power to balance them, were perpetually at variance." In the later centuries of the Middle Ages this lacuna became filled by the rise of a new group of people living in towns and involved in commercial activities. Clearly the idea of a mixed government comprising monarchical, aristocratic, and democratic elements had attraction for Robertson. But the essential feature of the notion of balance was for him that it implied the existence of counterweights inhibiting absolute control by one person or one class. Robertson abhorred despotism, which he regarded as characterized by the absence of any moderating or limiting institutions, whether they might be an independent judiciary or the privileges of hereditary nobility.

Improvement through adoption of rational principles was the criterion with which Robertson evaluated the developments of the past. In general these were ideas characteristic of the eighteenth century, and some of Robertson's passages read like an echo of statements by Montesquieu or Ferguson. However, the thinker whose influence on Robertson's thought is most clearly discernible was David Hume; Robertson's indebtedness to the discussions in Hume's *Essays Moral, Political and Literary* is obvious. Admittedly Robertson lacked the skeptical sharpness which allowed Hume to chart a rational course of action but also to appreciate the obstacles which man's passion placed in the way of realization of rational aims. But both Hume and Robertson were realists who accepted the basic soundness of the existing political world and stressed the need for the use of reason in the operation of its institutions. The task of enlightened men was improvement, not radical change.

Nevertheless, despite such agreements, there is also a difference between Hume's and Robertson's concept of history. The element which constituted this difference is important because it gives Robertson's approach to historical work a distinctive character. Robertson was a man of the church; his view of world history, in contrast to Hume's, was formed by Christian ideas. The religious assumptions of Robertson's concern with history were stated in a sermon which he preached in 1750 and which was then published, but to which, as far as I can see, students of Robertson's thought have given scant attention. This sermon has the title "The Situation of the World at the Time of Christ's Appearance and Its Connection with the Success of His Religion Considered." In accordance with this title Robertson described the political, moral, religious, and domestic situation which existed at the time of Christ's birth, and he stressed that in all these areas a point had been reached which favored the genesis and spread of Christianity. Robertson admitted that the topics which he discussed—political, moral, religious, and domestic developments—did not belong to the field of ecclesiastical or sacred history; the appropriate place was in what he called civil history and what we might call political history. The topics of these two genres of history differed: "Sacred history," Robertson said, "by drawing aside that veil which covers the councils of the Almighty, lays open His designs to the view of His creatures, and we can there trace the steps He taketh towards accomplishing them with more certainty and greater pleasure." But this direct revelation of God's will and purpose can come only from the study of ecclesiastical history, discussing sacred texts and the development of the church. All other areas of human activity belong to the field of civil history. However, this field too, although only in an indirect way, may make man aware "of the Divine wisdom in the government of the world." "Careful observers may often by the light of reason form probable conjectures with regard to the plan of God's providence and can discover a skillful hand directing the revolutions of human affairs, encompassing the best ends by the most effectual and surprising means."

The subjects with which ecclesiastical and civil history deal are different, but both have the purpose of discovering God's will. God's direction of human affairs shows itself in civil history by the gradual unfolding of a rational plan which the application of reason to the study of history will disclose to men. For Robertson, historical study, even if devoted to a single period, aimed at revealing the historical process as a whole; history was universal history, and this also in the sense that not one particular field of history (art or literature) but all history (political, moral, domestic) had to be studied in order to grasp God's plan. The writings of the philosophes, particularly of Voltaire, had given a fresh stimulus to the thinking about the problems of universal history, and Robertson had certainly absorbed some of their ideas on this subject; but he did not fully accept them. A sign of this is the somewhat ambiguous manner in which he referred to Voltaire in an appendix to his "View of the Progress of Society in Europe." Robertson acknowledged that Voltaire's essay *Sur l'Histoire Générale* had served as a "guide" in his researches, but he had not quoted him in his text because Voltaire had failed to cite the authorities from whom he derived his information. Robertson thought the foundations of Voltaire's work were weak; it placed too much of a burden on literary and artistic developments. For Robertson, progress was reflected not only in man's intellectual activities but in the entire process of history, and the task of the historian was to study society as a whole and to establish the facts of its development as carefully and accurately as possible, so that the presentation of the course of civil history would reveal the "skillful hand directing the revolutions of human affairs."

III

Robertson's historical method and his choice of historical topics were the natural result of his general approach to history. He worked hard at placing his histories on a reliable factual basis. He tried to construct his narration by means of contemporary documents and testimonies, but he was aware that these might be biased and ought not to be taken at their face value. He used private papers when possible, and if he relied chiefly on published and printed material, the reason was that he failed to gain access to the archives. It must be admitted that he did not make the sharp distinction between documentary and narrative sources which, since the adoption of the critical historical method in the nineteenth century, historians are wont to do. But Robertson had a strong feeling for the importance of primary material, and he looked at it with a critical eye. Although the philosophes had more interest in primary source material and more critical concern for its value than has frequently been assumed, it must be admitted that Gibbon and Robertson were exceptional in the seriousness of their efforts to lay hand on all the available source material and to use it cautiously and critically. Their works stand out from the historical writings of the philosophes because they were not only philosophical but also scholarly. In Gibbon's work the imagination of the philosophical historian was combined with the learning of the antiquarian, of the erudite who regarded everything ancient worth preserving. He collected all kinds of remains and had a particular interest in nonliterary sources. It has been said of Gibbon that his "novelty is to be found in the reconciliation of two historical methods rather than in a new interpretation of a historical period."

Robertson likewise reinforced philosophical history by the methods of a learned profession, but not, as in the case of Gibbon, that of the antiquarian. Robertson disdained the work of the antiquarian. In his *History of Scotland* he spoke of an early period which "is the region of pure fable and conjecture, and ought to be totally neglected or abandoned to the industry and credulity of antiquaries." Serious historical work could begin only where written sources, especially treatises and documents, were available; the learned profession which he combined with philosophical history was that of the legal historian.

Robertson learned about this approach in his student days at the University of Edinburgh. Until the nineteenth century, professorships devoted solely to the teaching of history were rare. Instruction in history was divided among the faculties. Ecclesiastical history was taught in the theological faculty, and legal history in the faculty of law. In addition it was expected that the professor of moral philosophy would use historical examples in his lectures on moral behavior. This was different, however, in Edinburgh, where since 1722 a professorship for universal civil history existed. Yet it is evident that, although the holder of this chair was not obligated to instruct in any particular branch of history, this professorship was meant to supplement instruction in ecclesiastical history, which had had a special chair in Edinburgh since 1702, and to fulfill those purposes for which at most other universities a chair in legal history was established. This is confirmed by the fact that the nominations for the chair in universal civil history at the University of Edinburgh were in the hands of the Faculties of Advocates. It is further underlined by the program for the lectures of the first holder of this chair, Charles Mackie, who announced that in his course on universal history he would discuss "remarkable passages in the 'Grand Corps Diplomatique,' Rymer's *Foedera* and other vouchers . . . taking occasion to detail any vulgar errors in history." Briefly, the great collections of public documents stating the rights and claims of European rulers and edited in a manner which critically examined their authenticity formed the basis of this course. Mackie was one of Robertson's favorite teachers, and the impact of the civil history which Robertson was taught in his student days can be seen in his emphasis on the value of written documents, the extensive use which he made of the great collection of treatises, his interest in the legal basis of social institutions, and his general scrutinizing attitude to sources. The situation which existed at the University of Edinburgh was also the source for the sharp separation of ecclesiastical and civil history which Robertson maintained throughout his life. It explains why, even in his treatment of the policy of Charles V, which was greatly influenced by religious conflicts, he hardly entered upon an analysis of the religious disputes and gave only a brief survey of the causes of the Reformation in pages which he himself called a "digression." Robertson's methodological innovations—the scholarly seriousness of his work—come from the combination of the approach of the learned jurist with the Enlightenment concepts of philosophical history.

IV

The various themes of Robertson's historical thought—consciousness of living in enlightened times, a sense for legal and institutional continuity, a Christian religiosity—played their part in his

decision to write on modern history. All his historical writings—
The History of Scotland (1759), *The History of the Reign of the
Emperor Charles V* (1769), and *The History of America* (1777),
which was intended to discuss an aspect of Charles V's rule which
he had omitted from the preceding work—dealt with the sixteenth century. This was an unusual choice. The preference of
the Enlightenment was for subjects that had to do with the classical world. When, after completion of the *History of Scotland*,
Robertson wrote to his friends asking their views about the
feasibility of a history of Charles V, their response was unfavor-
able. Horace Walpole wrote that Charles V was "a German or a
Spaniard and a foreigner could hardly comprehend the national
laws, customs and ideas" of these countries; he wanted Robertson
to write a history of Rome under the five good emperors which,
Walpole thought, would deserve the title "History of Humanity."
David Hume suggested to Robertson a biographical treatment of
modern rulers in the manner of Plutarch; about Robertson's
project of a history of Charles V, he said, "That subject is
disjointed; and your Hero, who is the sole connection is not very
interesting. . . . Though some parts of the story may be entertaining there would be many dry and barren; and the whole seems
not to have any great charms." But Robertson decided to go on
with his plan. Those whom he had consulted had not understood
that his interest in Charles V was not aroused by the personality
of the emperor but by the historical significance of the period in
which he ruled. In the preface of the work Robertson explained
why he regarded the sixteenth century as a crucial period of
European history, and this statement seemed to him so important
that he repeated it in similar words later on in the text of his
book: During the reign of Charles V "the powers of Europe were
formed into one great political system, in which each took a
station, wherein it has since remained with less variation, than
could have been expected after the shocks occasioned by so many
internal revolutions, and so many foreign wars. The great events
which happened then have not hitherto spent their force. The
political principles and maxims, then established, still continue
to operate. The ideas concerning the balance of power, then in-

troduced or rendered general, still influence the council of nations." It was Robertson's view that, in the sixteenth century, political life and particularly the conduct of foreign policy became organized according to rational principles, and that this period offered convincing proof for the belief that there is progress in world history, and disclosed the manner in which this progress was achieved. It was an age that could serve as an elevating example of the working of "Divine wisdom in the government of the world."

Of course, Robertson was not the first in assigning to this period great historical significance. Voltaire had declared that the time of the Medici in Florence had been one of the four periods of history in which a man of thought or taste could have led a happy life. The fifteenth and sixteenth centuries, with their "renaissance des lettres et des beaux arts" represented a decisive step towards the development of a more enlightened world. Two main features of Robertson's thought—the interconnected nature of European foreign policy and the notion of balance of power—had been emphasized by Guicciardini, whom Robertson regarded as "the most sagacious perhaps of all modern historians," and on whom he relied heavily in his *History of the Reign of Charles V*. In detail, however, Guicciardini's interpretation deviated from Robertson because for Guicciardini the struggle between Charles V and Francis I ended the peaceful and prosperous state which had existed in Italy in the fifteenth century when the Italian statesmen had carefully observed the principle of balance of power; in Guicciardini's view the sixteenth century was a decline from the fifteenth century rather than a step forward. Bolingbroke too had directed attention to the importance of the sixteenth century. In his *Letters on the Study and Use of History* he called "the sixteenth century fruitful of great events and of astonishing revolutions," and he was one of the chief writers who advocated the importance of the principle of balance of power. Yet, insofar as his work contained any historical descriptions of significance—most of them were aphoristic and superficial—they bear on developments of the seventeenth and eighteenth century.

It is doubtful, however, that these reflections from the spheres of the history of civilization and of diplomacy would have weighed as heavily with Robertson as the thought that the sixteenth century was the age of the Reformation. Explanation and analysis of the political importance of the age whose significance in religious history was obvious must have appeared to him a most desirable and necessary task. For although ecclesiastical history and civil history had different content and were to be kept separate, they moved along parallel lines.

Although the component parts might have been extant elsewhere, there remains originality in the sharpness and clarity with which Robertson represented the sixteenth century as creating an interconnected European state system, thus ushering in the history of modern times. Although there are great differences, there is also a fundamental similarity between Robertson's views and that view of the nature of the history of the modern world which, through the work of Ranke, became an integral element in the conceptual structure of the historiography of the nineteenth century. Yet because Robertson offered more than the history of the reign of a particular ruler, because he tried to show what the distinguishing and permanent features of the European political world in modern times were, the section titled "A View of the Progress of Society in Europe," with which the work opens, is more than an introduction that, in the pattern of the ancient historians, surveys the political situation which existed at the time the writer began his history. Robertson's introduction was intended to show how, out of raw and primitive beginnings, the forces arose which made a civilized and enlightened world possible. It is a reflection on the factors which have determined the character of the European world.

When the work of a historian is given its place in the development of historiography, its value will almost unavoidably be lowered; the mere fact that historical scholarship continues its researches makes the historical works of former periods obsolete. The application of modern scholarly criteria to the historical works of the eighteenth century is particularly unfair because the authors of these works did not intend to be purely scholars; they regarded themselves as literati, and they wanted to produce works of literature. In the eighteenth century, historical writing was one of the most popular literary genres, and the earnings of a successful historical writer could be considerable. In the letter in which David Hume tried to dissuade Robertson from writing a history of Charles V, financial considerations played a considerable role. Hume expected that a book in the manner of Plutarch would make a considerable sum of money, while he doubted that a life of Charles V would arouse much interest. In this he was wrong. The success of the *History of the Reign of Charles V* was immense. Robertson received the then very large sum of £4,500 for his work.

The eighteenth-century public chiefly valued the literary qualities of these histories, and the historical writings of Hume, Gibbon, and Robertson enjoyed great reputation because their authors were regarded as "elegant" writers. This view, I believe, will be shared by today's reader. It is astonishing how smoothly the pages of Robertson's "View of the Progress of Society in Europe" read, although they deal neither with persons nor with exciting events, but with an analysis of institutional developments and political structures. Yet not only the form of presentation but also the contents deserve our attention—and not only because of the influence of this work on the development of historiography. We might now smile about Robertson's characterization of the Crusades as a "monument of human folly" or about his condemnation of scholastic theology as a "vain philosophy." But we soon become aware that in many passages Robertson stated frankly and starkly what are still our views or prejudices about the forces working in history. In showing us the extent to which our attitudes are still formed by the past and in inviting us to self-criticism, Robertson's work can still fulfill a useful and needed function.

Textual and Bibliographical Note

THE text of Robertson's "A View of the Progress of Society in Europe from the Subversion of the Roman Empire to the Beginning of the Sixteenth Century" is given as it was printed in the first edition of his *The History of the Reign of the Emperor Charles V*, published in London in 1769. Of the forty-four proofs and illustrations which follow the "View of the Progress of Society in Europe," only three are reproduced. The symbols indicating the existence of "proofs and illustrations" for particular points have therefore been removed. Footnotes have been added indicating the locations of the three proofs that have been retained. In his footnotes Robertson usually gives the titles of works to which he referred in an abbreviated form, and this form of citation presents difficulties to the modern reader. Because a student of historiography might find Robertson's references to the historical literature of the eighteenth century instructive, the footnotes have been changed to give the full titles of the works quoted. If in the proofs and illustrations, which have no footnotes, previously unmentioned titles are given in an abbreviated form, the full title will be noted in the index.

The first collection of Robertson's works appeared between 1800 and 1802 in eleven volumes and was followed by many further editions of his works. The basic biography is by Dugald Stewart, *Account of the Life and Writings of William Robertson* (London, 1801). This biography was also printed as in introduction to some of the editions of Robertson's works; others are prefaced by a biography by R. Lyman which contains some additional facts on Robertson's life. Further biographical material is listed in the bibliography following the description of Robertson's life in the *DEB*. In recent years Manfred Schlenke has studied Robertson's papers and has published the results of his researches in two articles:"Kulturgeschichte oder politische Geschichte in der Geschichtsschreibung des 18. Jahrhunderts; William Robertson als Historiker des europäischen Staatensystem," *Archiv für Kulturgeschichte* 37 (1955): 60–97; and "Aus der Frühzeit des englischen Historismus; William Robertsons Beitrag zur methodischen Grundlegung der Geschichtswissenschaft im 18. Jahrhundert," *Saeculum* 7 (1956): 107–25. Schlenke's studies try to determine Robertson's place in the intellectual history of the eighteenth century; brief similar discussions of Robertson as representative of the historical thought of the Enlightenment can be found in most works dealing with the Enlightenment or with the development of historiography. The most significant are J. B. Black, *The Art of History* (New York, 1926); Friedrich Meinecke, *Die Entstehung des Historismus* (Munich, 1959); Peter Gay, *The Enlightenment: An Interpretation,* 2 vols. (New York, 1969). For an understanding of the problems of the eighteenth-century historiography two articles by Arnaldo Momigliano, "Ancient History and the Antiquarian" and "Gibbon's Contribution to Historical Method," now published in A. D. Momigliano, *Studies in Historiography* (New York, 1966), are crucial.

In almost all these general discussions Robertson is somewhat overshadowed by Hume and Gibbon, and Robertson's important role in Scottish intellectual life is slighted. For this aspect of Robertson's activities and interests see the histories of the University of Edinburgh by Sir Alexander Grant, 2 vols., 1884, and by D. B. Horn, *A Short History of the University of Edinburgh 1556–1899* (Edinburgh, 1967). The first volume of Andrew Dalzel, *History of the University of Edinburgh* (Edinburgh, 1862), containing memoirs and letters, is valuable for an understanding of Robertson's personality. *The Autobiography of the Rev. Dr. Alexander*

Carlyle, edited by J. H. Burton (Edinburgh and London, 1861), contains a revealing characterization of Robertson, as it does of all the leaders of the Scottish Renaissance. For the general background see *Scotland in the Age of Improvement,* edited by N. T. Philipson and Rosalind Mitchison (Edinburgh, 1970).

A VIEW OF THE PROGRESS
OF SOCIETY IN EUROPE

Preface to the History of the Reign of the Emperor Charles V

No period in the history of one's own country can be considered as altogether uninteresting. Such transactions as tend to illustrate the progress of its constitution, laws, or manners, merit the utmost attention. Even remote and minute events are objects of a curiosity, which, being natural to the human mind, the gratification of it is attended with pleasure.

But with respect to the history of foreign states, we must set other bounds to our desire of information. The universal progress of science during the last two centuries, the art of printing, and other obvious causes, have filled Europe with such a multiplicity of histories, and with such vast collections of historical materials, that the term of human life is too short for the study or even the perusal of them. It is necessary, then, not only for those who are called to conduct the affairs of nations, but for such as inquire and reason concerning them, to remain satisfied with a general knowledge of distant events, and to confine their study of history in detail chiefly to that period, in which the several States of Europe having become intimately connected, the operations of one power so felt by all, as to influence their councils, and to regulate their measures.

Some boundary, then, ought to be fixed in order to separate these periods. An æra should be pointed out, prior to which, each country, little connected with those around it, may trace its own history apart; after which, the transactions of every considerable nation in Europe become interesting and instructive to all. With this intention I undertook to write the history of the Emperor Charles V. It was during his administration that the powers of Europe were formed into one great political system, in which each took a station, wherein it has since remained with less variation, than could have been expected after the shocks occasioned by so many internal revolutions, and so many foreign wars. The great events which happened then have not hitherto spent their force. The political principles and maxims, then established, still continue to operate. The ideas concerning the balance of power, then introduced or rendered general, still influence the councils of nations.

The age of Charles V may therefore be considered as the period at which the political state of Europe began to assume a new form. I have endeavoured to render my account of it, an introduction to the history of Europe subsequent to his reign. While his numerous Biographers describe his personal qualities and actions; while the historians of different countries relate occurrences the consequences of which were local or transient, it hath been my purpose to record only those great transactions in his reign, the effects of which were universal, or continue to be permanent.

As my readers could derive little instruction from such a history of the reign of Charles V without some information concerning the state of Europe previous to the sixteenth century, my desire of supplying this has produced a preliminary volume, in which I have attempted to point out and explain the great causes and events, to whose operation all the improvements in the political state of Europe, from the subversion of the Roman Empire to the beginning of the sixteenth century, must be ascribed. I have exhibited a view of the progress of society in Europe, not only with respect to interior government, laws and manners, but with respect to the command of the national force requisite in foreign operations; and I have described the political constitution of the principal states in Europe at the time when Charles V began his reign.

In this part of my work I have been led into several critical disquisitions, which belong more properly to the province of the lawyer or antiquary, than to that of the historian. These I have placed at the end of the first volume, under the title of Proofs and Illustrations. Many of my readers will, probably, give little attention to such researches. To some they may, perhaps, appear the most curious and interesting part of the work. I have carefully pointed out the sources from which I have derived information, and have cited the writers on whose authority I rely with a minute exactness, which might appear to border upon ostentation, if it were possible to be vain of having read books, many of which nothing but the duty of examining with accuracy whatever I laid before the publick, could have induced me to open. As my inquiries conducted me often into paths which were obscure or little frequented, such constant recourse to the authors who have been my guides, was not only necessary for authenticating the facts which are the foundations of my reasonings, but may be useful in pointing out the way to such as shall hereafter hold the same course, and in enabling them to carry on their researches with greater facility and success.

Every intelligent reader will observe one omission in my work, the reason of which it is necessary to explain. I have given no account of the conquests of Mexico and Peru, or of the establishment of the Spanish colonies in the continent and islands of America. The history of these events I originally intended to have related at considerable length. But upon a nearer and more attentive consideration of this part of my plan, I found that the discovery of the new world; the state of society among its ancient inhabitants; their character, manners, and arts; the genius of the European settlements in its various provinces, together with the influence of these upon the systems of policy or commerce in Europe, were subjects so splendid and important, that a superficial view of them could afford little satisfaction; to treat of them as extensively as they merited, must produce an episode, disproportionate to the principle work. I have therefore reserved these for a separate history; which, if the performance now offered to the publick shall receive its approbation, I propose to undertake.

Though, by omitting such considerable but detached articles in the reign of Charles V I have circumscribed my narration within more narrow limits, I am yet persuaded, from this view of the intention and nature of the work which I thought it necessary to lay before my readers, that the plan must still appear to them too extensive, and the undertaking too arduous. I have often felt them to be so. But my conviction of the utility of such a history prompted me to persevere. With what success I have executed it, the publick must now judge. I wait, in sollicitude, for its decision; to which I shall submit with a respectful silence.

I

Interior Government, Laws and Manners

Two great revolutions have happened in the political state, and in the manners of the European nations. The first was occasioned by the progress of the Roman power; the second by the subversion of the Roman Empire. When the spirit of conquest led the armies of Rome beyond the Alps, they found all the countries which they invaded, inhabited by people whom they denominated barbarians, but who were nevertheless brave and independant. These defended their ancient possessions with obstinate valour. It was by the superiority of their discipline, rather than of their courage, that the Romans gained any advantage over them. A single battle did not, as among the effeminate inhabitants of Asia, decide the fate of a state. The vanquished people resumed their arms with fresh spirit, and their undisciplined valour, animated by the love of liberty, supplied the want of conduct as well as of union. During these long and fierce struggles for dominion or independance, the countries of Europe were successively laid waste, a great part of their inhabitants perished in the field, many were carried into slavery, and a feeble remnant, incapable of further resistance, submitted to the Roman power.

The Romans having thus desolated Europe, set themselves to civilize it. The form of government which they established in the conquered provinces, though severe, was regular, and preserved public tranquillity. As a consolation for the loss of liberty, they communicated their arts, sciences, language, and manners, to their new subjects. Europe began to breathe, and to recover strength after the calamities which it had undergone; agriculture was encouraged; population encreased; the ruined cities were rebuilt; new towns were founded; an appearance of prosperity succeeded, and repaired, in some degree, the havock of war.

This state, however, was far from being happy, or favourable to the improvement of the human mind. The vanquished nations were disarmed by their conquerors, and overawed by soldiers kept in pay to restrain them. They were given up as a prey to rapacious governors, who plundered them with impunity; and were drained of their wealth by exorbitant taxes, imposed with so little attention to the situation of the provinces, that the impositions were generally increased in proportion to their inability to support them. They were deprived of their most enterprizing citizens, who resorted to a distant capital in quest of preferment, or of riches; and were accustomed in all their actions to look up to a superior, and tamely to receive his commands. Under all these depressing circumstances, it was impossible that they could retain vigour or generosity of mind. The martial and independant spirit, which had distinguished their ancestors, became extinct among all the people subjected to the Roman yoke; they lost not only the habit but even the capacity of deciding for themselves, or of acting from the impulse of their own minds; and the dominion of the Romans, like that of all great Empires, degraded and debased the human species.

A society in this state could not subsist long. There were defects in the Roman government, even in its most perfect form, which threatened its dissolution. Time ripened these original feeds of corruption, and gave birth to many new disorders. A constitution, unfounded, and worn out, must have fallen in pieces of itself, without any external shock. The violent irruption of the Goths, Vandals, Huns, and other barbarians hastened this event, and precipitated the downfal of the Empire. New nations seemed to arise, and to rush from unknown regions in order to take vengeance on the Romans for the calamities which they had inflicted on mankind. These fierce tribes either inhabited the various provinces in Germany which had never been subdued by the Romans, or were scattered over the vast countries in the north of Europe, and north-west of Asia, which are now occupied by the Danes, the Swedes, the Poles, the subjects of the Russian empire, and the Tartars. Their condition, and transactions previous to their invasion of the Empire are but little known. All our information with respect to these is derived from the Romans; and as they did not penetrate far into countries which were at that time uncultivated and uninviting, the accounts of their original state given by them are extremely imperfect. The rude inhabitants themselves, destitute of science, and of records, without leisure, or curiosity to enquire into remote events, retained, perhaps, some indistinct memory of recent occurrences, but beyond these, all was buried in oblivion, or involved in darkness, and in fable.

The prodigious swarms which poured in upon the Empire from the beginning of the fourth century to the final extinction of the Roman power, have given rise to an opinion that the countries whence they issued were crowded with inhabitants; and various theories have been formed to account for such an extraordinary degree of population as hath procured these countries the appellation of The Storehouse of Nations. But if we consider that the countries possessed by the people who invaded the Empire were of vast extent; that a great part of these was covered with woods and marshes; that some of the most considerable of the barbarous nations subsisted entirely by hunting or pasturage, in both which states of society large tracts of land are required for maintaining a few inhabitants; and that all of them were strangers to the arts, and industry, without which population cannot increase to any great degree, it is evident, that these countries could not be so populous in ancient times as they are at present, when they still continue to be less peopled than any other part of Europe or of Asia.

But if these circumstances prevented the barbarous nations from becoming populous, they contributed to inspire, or to strengthen the martial spirit by which they were distinguished.

9

Inured by the rigour of their climate, or the poverty of their soil, to hardships which rendered their bodies firm, and their minds vigorous; accustomed to a course of life which was a continual preparation for action; and disdaining every occupation but that of war; they undertook, and prosecuted their military enterprizes with an ardour and impetuosity, of which men softened by the refinements of more polished times, can scarce form any idea.

Their first inroads into the Empire proceeded rather from the love of plunder, than from the desire of new settlements. Roused to arms by some enterprizing or popular leader, they sallied out of their forests; broke in upon the frontier provinces with irresistible violence; put all who opposed them to the sword; carried off the most valuable effects of the inhabitants; dragged along multitudes of captives in chains; wasted all before them with fire or sword; and returned in triumph to their wilds and fastnesses. Their success, together with the accounts which they gave of the unknown conveniencies and luxuries that abounded in countries better cultivated, or blessed with a milder climate than their own, excited new adventurers, and exposed the frontier to new devastations.

When nothing was left to plunder in the adjacent provinces ravaged by frequent incursions, they marched farther from home, and finding it difficult, or dangerous to return, they began to settle in the countries which they had subdued. The sudden and short excursions in quest of booty, which had alarmed, and disquieted the Empire, ceased; a more dreadful calamity impended. Great bodies of armed men with their wives and children, and slaves and flocks, issued forth, like regular colonies, in quest of new settlements. People who had no cities, and seldom any fixed habitation, were so little attached to their native soil, that they migrated without reluctance from one place to another. New adventurers followed them. The lands which they deserted were occupied by more remote tribes of barbarians. These, in their turn, pushed forward into more fertile countries, and like a torrent continually increasing, rolled on, and swept every thing before them. In less than two centuries from their first irruption, barbarians of various names and lineage, plundered and took pos-

10

session of Thrace, Pannonia, Gaul, Spain, Africa, and at last of Italy, and Rome itself. The vast fabrick of the Roman power which it had been the work of ages to perfect, was in that short period overturned from the foundation.

Many concurring causes prepared the way for this great revolution, and ensured success to the nations which invaded the Empire. The Roman commonwealth had conquered the world by the wisdom of its civil maxims, and the rigour of its military discipline. But, under the Emperors, the former were forgotten or despised, and the latter was gradually relaxed. The armies of the Empire in the fourth and fifth centuries bore scarce any resemblance to those invincible legions which had been victorious wherever they marched. Instead of freemen, who voluntarily took arms from the love of glory, or of their country, provincials and barbarians were bribed or forced into service. They were too feeble, or too proud to submit to the fatigue of military duty. They even complained of the weight of their defensive armour, as intolerable, and laid it aside. Infantry, from which the armies of ancient Rome derived their vigour and stability, fell into contempt; the effeminate and undisciplined soldiers of later times could scarce be brought to venture into the field but on horseback. These wretched troops, however, were the only guardians of the empire. The jealousy of despotism had deprived the people of the use of arms; and subjects oppressed and rendered incapable of defending themselves, had neither spirit nor inclination to resist their invaders, from whom they had little to fear, because they could scarce make their condition more unhappy. As the martial spirit became extinct, the revenues of the Empire gradually diminished. The taste for the luxuries of the East increased to such a pitch in the Imperial court, that great sums were carried into India, from which money never returns. By the vast subsidies paid to the barbarous nations a still greater quantity of species was withdrawn from circulation. The frontier provinces wasted by frequent incursions became unable to pay the customary tribute; and the wealth of the world, which had long centered in the capital of the Empire, ceased to flow thither in the same abundance, or was diverted into other channels. The limits of the Empire continued to be as extensive as ever, while the spirit requisite for its defence declined, and its resources were exhausted. A vast body, languid, and almost unanimated, became incapable of any effort to save itself, and was easily overpowered. The Emperors, who had the absolute direction of this disordered system, sunk in the softness of Eastern luxury, shut up within the walls of a palace, ignorant of war, unacquainted with affairs, and governed entirely by women and eunuchs, or by ministers equally effeminate, trembled at the approach of danger, and under circumstances which called for the utmost vigour in counsel as well as in action, discovered all the impotent irresolution of fear, and of folly.

In every respect, the condition of the barbarous nations was the reverse of that of the Romans. Among them, the martial spirit was in full vigour; their leaders were hardy and enterprizing; the arts which had enervated the Romans were unknown among them; and such was the nature of their military institutions, that they brought forces into the field without any trouble, and supported them at little expence. The mercenary and effeminate troops stationed on the frontier, astonished at their fierceness, either fled at their approach, or were routed in the first onset. The feeble expedient to which the Emperors had recourse, of taking large bodies of the barbarians into pay, and of employing them to repel new invaders, instead of retarding, hastened the destruction of the Empire. They soon turned their arms against their masters, and with greater advantage than ever: for, by serving in the Roman armies, they had acquired all the discipline, or skill in war, which the Romans still retained; and upon adding these to their native ferocity, they became altogether irresistible.

But though from these, and many other causes, the progress and conquests of the nations which over-ran the Empire, became so extremely rapid, they were accompanied with horrible devastations, and an incredible destruction of the human species. Civilized nations which take arms upon cool reflection, from motives of policy or prudence, with a view to guard against some distant danger, or to prevent some remote contingency, carry on their hostilities with so little rancour, or animosity, that war among

12

them is disarmed of half its terrors. Barbarians are strangers to such refinements. They rush into war with impetuosity, and prosecute it with violence. Their sole object is to make their enemies feel the weight of their vengeance, nor does their rage subside until it be satiated with inflicting on them every possible calamity. It is with such a spirit that the savage tribes in America carry on their petty wars. It was with the same spirit that the more powerful and no less fierce barbarians in the north of Europe, and of Asia, fell upon the Roman Empire.

Wherever they marched, their rout was marked with blood. They ravaged or destroyed all around them. They made no distinction between what was sacred, and what was profane. They respected no age, or sex, or rank. What escaped the fury of the first inundation perished in those which followed it. The most fertile and populous provinces were converted into deserts, in which were scattered the ruins of villages and cities, that afforded shelter to a few miserable inhabitants whom chance had preserved, or the sword of the enemy, wearied with destroying, had spared. The conquerors who first settled in the countries which they had wasted were expelled or exterminated by new invaders, who coming from regions farther removed from the civilized parts of the world, were still more fierce and rapacious. This brought new calamities upon mankind, which did not cease until the north, by pouring forth successive swarms, was drained of people, and could no longer furnish instruments of destruction. Famine and pestilence, which always march in the train of war, when it ravages with such inconsiderate cruelty, raged in every part of Europe, and compleated its sufferings. If a man were called to fix upon the period in the history of the world, during which the condition of the human race was most calamitous and afflicted, he would without hesitation, name that which elapsed from the death of Theodosius the Great, to the establishment of the Lombards in Italy.[1] The contemporary authors who beheld that scene of desolation, labour and are at a loss for expressions to describe the horror of it. *The scourge of God, The destroyer of nations,* are the dreadful epithets by which they distinguished the most noted of the barbarous leaders; and they compared the ruin which they had brought on the world, to the havock occasioned by earth-quakes, conflagrations, or deluges, the most formidable and fatal calamities which the imagination of man can conceive.

But no expressions can convey so perfect an idea of the destructive progress of the barbarians as that which must strike an attentive observer, when he contemplates the total change, which he will discover in the state of Europe when it began to recover some degree of tranquillity towards the close of the sixth century. The Saxons were by that time masters of the southern, and more fertile provinces of Britain; the Franks of Gaul; the Huns of Pannonia; the Goths of Spain; the Goths and Lombards of Italy and the adjacent provinces. Scarce any vestige of the Roman policy, jurisprudence, arts, or literature, remained. New forms of government, new laws, new manners, new dresses, new languages, and new names of men and countries, were every where introduced. To make a great or sudden alteration with respect to any of these, unless where the ancient inhabitants of a country have been almost totally exterminated, has proved an undertaking beyond the power of the greatest conquerors. The total change which the settlement of the barbarous nations occasioned in the state of Europe, may, therefore, be considered as a more decisive proof, than even the testimony of contemporary historians, of the destructive violence with which they carried on their conquests, and of the havock which they had made from one extremity of this quarter of the globe to the other.

In the obscurity of the chaos occasioned by this general wreck of nations, we must search for the seeds of order, and endeavour to discover the first rudiments of the policy and laws now established in Europe. To this source, the historians of its different kingdoms, have attempted, though with less attention and industry than the importance of the enquiry merits, to trace back the institutions, and customs peculiar to their countrymen. It is not my province to give a minute detail of the progress of government and manners in each particular nation, whose transactions are the object of the following history. But in order to exhibit a just view of the state of Europe at the opening of the sixteenth century, it is necessary to look back, and to contemplate the condition of the northern nations upon their first settlement in those countries which they occupied. It is necessary to mark the great steps by which they advanced from barbarism to refinement, and to point out those general principles and events which by their uniform as well as extensive operation conducted all of them to that degree of improvement in policy and in manners which they had attained at the period when Charles V began his reign.

When nations subject to despotic government make conquests, these serve only to extend the dominion and the power of their master. But armies composed of freemen conquer for themselves, not for their leaders. The people who overturned the Roman Empire, and settled in its various provinces, were of the latter class. Not only the different nations that issued from the north of Europe, which has always been considered as the seat of liberty, but the Huns and Alans who inhabited part of those countries which have been marked out as the peculiar region of servitude,[2] enjoyed freedom and independance to such a high degree as seems to be scarce compatible with a state of social union, or with the subordination necessary to maintain it. They followed the chieftain who led them forth in quest of new settlements, not by constraint, but from choice; not as soldiers whom he could order to march, but as volunteers who offered to accompany him.* They considered their conquests as a common property, in which all had a title to share, as all had contributed to acquire them. In what manner, or by what principles, they divided among them the lands which they seized, we cannot now determine with any certainty. There is no nation in Europe whose records reach back to this remote period; and there is little information to be got from the uninstructive and meagre chronicles, compiled by writers ignorant of the true end, and unacquainted with the proper objects of history.

This new division of property, however, together with the maxims and manners to which it gave rise, gradually introduced a species of government formerly unknown. This singular institution is now distinguished by the name of the *Feudal system:* and

* See note beginning on p. 149, Proofs and Illustrations.—Editor.

though the barbarous nations which framed it, settled in their new territories at different times, came from different countries, spoke various languages, and were under the command of separate leaders, the Feudal policy and laws were established, with little variation, in every kingdom of Europe. This amazing uniformity hath induced some authors[3] to believe that all these nations, notwithstanding so many apparent circumstances of distinction, were originally the same people. But it may be ascribed with greater probability to the similar state of society and of manner to which they were assustomed in their native countries, and to the similar situation in which they found themselves on taking possession of their new domains.

As the conquerors of Europe had their acquisitions to maintain, not only against such of the ancient inhabitants as they had spared, but against the more formidable inroads of new invaders, self-defense was their chief care, and seems to have been the sole object of their first institution and policy. Instead of those loose associations, which, though they scarce diminished their personal independance, had been sufficient for their security while they remained in their original countries, they saw the necessity of confederating more closely together, and of relinquishing some of their private rights in order to attain publick safety. Every freeman, upon receiving a portion of the lands which were divided, bound himself to appear in arms against the enemies of the community. This military service was the condition upon which he received and held his lands, and as they were exempted from every other burden, that tenure, among a warlike people, was deemed both easy and honourable. The King or general, who led them to conquest, continuing still to be the head of the colony, had, of course, the largest portion allotted to him. Having thus acquired the means of rewarding past services, as well as of gaining new adherents, he parcelled out his lands with this view, binding those on whom they were bestowed, to follow his standard with a number of men in proportion to the extent of the territory, which they received, and to bear arms in his defence. His chief officers imitated the example of the sovereign, and in distributing portions of their lands among their dependants, annexed the same condition to the grant. Thus a feudal kingdom resembled a military establishment, rather than a civil institution. The victorious army cantoned out in the country which it had seized, continued ranged under its proper officers, and subordinate to military command. The names of a soldier and of a freeman were synonimous.[4] Every proprietor of land, girt with a sword, was ready to march at the summons of his superior, and to take the field against the common enemy.

But though the Feudal policy seems to be so admirably calculated for defence against the assaults of any foreign power, its provisions for the interior order and tranquillity of society were extremely defective. The principles of disorder and corruption are discernable in that constitution under its best and most perfect form. They soon unfolded themselves, and spreading with rapidity through every part of the system, produced the most fatal effects. The bond of political union was extremely feeble; the sources of anarchy were innumerable. The monarchical and aristocratical parts of the constitution, having no intermediate power to balance them, were perpetually at variance, and justling with each other. The powerful vassals of the crown soon extorted a confirmation for life of those grants of land, which being at first purely gratuitous, had been bestowed only during pleasure. Not satisfied with this, they prevailed to have them converted into hereditary possessions. One step more compleated their usurpations, and rendered them unalienable.* With an ambition no less enterprizing, and more preposterous, they appropriated to themselves titles of honour, as well as offices of power or trust. These personal marks of distinction, which the publick admiration bestows on illustrious merit, or which the publick confidence confers on extraordinary abilities, were annexed to certain families, and transmitted like fiefs, from father to son by hereditary right. The crown vassals having thus secured the possession of their lands and dignities, the nature of the Feudal institutions, which though founded in subordination, verged to independance, led them to new, and still more dangerous encroachments on the prerogatives of the sovereign. They obtained the power of supreme jurisdiction both civil and criminal within their own

* See note beginning on p. 154, Proofs and Illustrations.—EDITOR.

territories; the right of coining money; together with the privilege of carrying on war against their private enemies in their own name, and by their own authority. The ideas of political subjection were almost entirely lost, and frequently scarce any appearance of feudal subordination remained. Nobles who had acquired such enormous power, scorned to consider themselves as subjects. They aspired openly at being independant: the bonds which connected the principal members of the constitution with the crown, were dissolved. A kingdom considerable in name and in extent, was broken into as many separate principalities as it contained powerful barons. A thousand causes of jealousy and discord subsisted among them, and gave rise to as many wars. Every country in Europe, wasted or kept in continual alarm during these endless contests, was filled with castles and places of strength, erected for the security of the inhabitants, not against foreign force, but against internal hostilities. An universal anarchy, destructive, in a great measure, of all the advantages which men expect to derive from society, prevailed. The people, the most numerous as well as the most useful part of the community, were either reduced to a state of actual servitude, or treated with the same insolence and rigour as if they had been degraded into that wretched condition. The King, stripped of almost every prerogative, and without authority to enact or to execute salutary laws, could neither protect the innocent, nor punish the guilty. The nobles, superior to all restraint, harrassed each other with perpetual wars, oppressed their fellow subjects and humbled or insulted their sovereign. To crown all, time gradually fixed, and rendered venerable this pernicious system which violence had established.

Such was the state of Europe with respect to the interior administration of government from the seventh to the eleventh century. All the external operations of its various states, during this period, were, of course, extremely feeble. A kingdom dismembered, and torn with dissention, without any common interest to rouze, or any common head to conduct its force, was incapable of acting with vigour. Almost all the wars in Europe, during the ages which I have mentioned, were trifling, indecisive, and pro-

ductive of no considerable event. They resembled the short incursions of pirates or banditti, rather than the steady operations
of a regular army. Every baron at the head of his vassals, carried
on some petty enterprize to which he was prompted by his own
ambition, or revenge. The state itself, destitute of union, either
remained altogether inactive, or if it attempted to make any effort,
that served only to discover its impotence. The superior genius
of Charlemagne, it is true, united all these disjointed and discordant members, and forming them again into one body, restored
that degree of activity to government which distinguish his reign,
and render the transactions of it, objects not only of attention but
of admiration to more enlightened times. But this state of union
and vigour not being natural to the feudal government, was of
short duration. Immediately upon his death, the spirit which
animated and sustained the vast system which he had established,
being withdrawn, it broke into pieces. All the calamities which
flow from anarchy and discord, returning with additional force,
afflicted the different kingdoms into which his Empire was split.
From that time to the eleventh century, a succession of uninteresting events; a series of wars, the motives as well as the consequences of which were equally unimportant, fill and deform the
annals of all the nations in Europe.

To these pernicious effects of the feudal anarchy, may be added
its fatal influence on the character and improvement of the human
mind. If men do not enjoy the protection of regular government,
together with the certainty of personal security which naturally
flows from it, they never attempt to make progress in science,
nor aim at attaining refinement in taste, or in manners. That
period of turbulence, oppression, and rapine, which I have described, was ill suited to favour improvement in any of these. In
less than a century after the barbarous nations settled in their new
conquests, almost all the effects of the knowledge and civility
which the Romans had spread through Europe disappeared. Not
only the arts of elegance which minister to luxury, and are supported by it, but many of the useful arts, without which life can
scarce be considered as comfortable, were neglected or lost.
Literature, science, taste, were words scarce in use during the

ages we are contemplating; or if they occur at any time, eminence in them is ascribed to persons and productions so contemptible that it appears their true import was little understood. Persons of the highest rank, and in the most eminent stations could not read or write. Many of the clergy did not understand the breviary which they were obliged daily to recite; some of them could scarce read it. All memory of past transactions was lost, or preserved in annals filled with trifling events, or legendary tales. Even the codes of laws published by the several nations which established themselves in the different countries of Europe, fell into disuse, while in their place, customs, vague and capricious, were substituted. The human mind neglected, uncultivated, and depressed, sunk into the most profound ignorance. Europe did not produce, during four centuries, one author who merits to be read, either on account of the elegance of his composition, or the justness and novelty of his sentiments. There is scarce one invention useful or ornamental to society of which that long period can boast.

Even the Christian religion, though its precepts are delivered, and its institutions are fixed in scripture with a precision which should exempted them from being misinterpreted or corrupted, degenerated during those ages of darkness into an illiberal superstition. The barbarous nations when converted to Christianity changed the object, not the spirit of their religious worship. They endeavoured to conciliate the favour of the true God by means not unlike to those which they had employed in order to appease their false deities. Instead of aspiring to sanctity and virtue, which alone can render men acceptable to the great author of order and of excellence, they imagined that they satisfied every obligation of duty by a scrupulous observance of external ceremonies. Religion, according to their conception of it, comprehended nothing else; and the rites, by which they persuaded themselves that they could gain the favour of heaven, were of such a nature as might have been expected from the rude ideas of the ages which devised and introduced them. They were either so unmeaning as to be altogether unworthy of the Being to whose honour they were consecrated; or so absurd as to be a disgrace to reason and humanity. Charlemagne in France, and Alfred the Great in England, endeavoured to dispel this darkness, and gave their subjects a short glimpse of light and knowledge. But the ignorance of the age was too powerful for their efforts and institutions. The darkness returned, and settled over Europe more thick and heavy than formerly.

As the inhabitants of Europe during these centuries were strangers to the arts which embellish a polished age, they were destitute of the virtues which abound among people who continue in a simple state. Force of mind, a sense of personal dignity, gallantry in enterprize, invincible perseverance in execution, and contempt of danger and of death, are the characteristic virtues of uncivilized nations. But these are all the offspring of equality and independance, both which the feudal institutions had destroyed. The spirit of domination corrupted the nobles; the yoke of servitude depressed the people; the generous sentiments inspired by a sense of equality were extinguished, and nothing remained to be a check on ferocity and violence. Human society is in its most corrupted state at that period when men have lost their original independance and simplicity of manners, but have not attained that degree of refinement which introduces a sense of decorum and of propriety in conduct, as a restraint on those passions which lead to heinous crimes. Accordingly, a greater number of those atrocious actions which fill the mind of man with astonishment and horror, occur in the history of the centuries under review, than in that of any period of the same extent in the annals of Europe. If we open the history of Gregory of Tours, or of any contemporary author, we meet with a series of deeds of cruelty, perfidy, and revenge, so wild and enormous as almost to exceed belief.

But, according to the observation of an elegant and profound historian,[5] there is an ultimate point of depression, as well as of exaltation, from which human affairs naturally return in a contrary progress, and beyond which they seldom pass either in their advancement or decline. When defects, either in the form, or in the administration of government, occasion such disorders in society as are excessive and intolerable, it becomes the common interest to discover and to apply such remedies as will most effectually remove them. Slight inconveniences may be long overlooked or endured, but when abuses grow to a certain pitch, the society must go to ruin, or must attempt to reform them. The disorders in the feudal system, together with the corruption of taste and manner consequent upon these, which had gone on increasing during a long course of years, seem to have attained their utmost point of excess towards the close of the eleventh century. From that æra, we may date the return of government and manners in a contrary direction, and can trace a succession of causes and events which contributed, some with a nearer and more powerful, others with a more remote and less perceptible influence, to abolish confusion and barbarism, and to introduce order, regularity, and refinement.

In pointing out and explaining these causes and events, it is not necessary to observe the order of time with a chronological accuracy; it is of more importance to keep in view their mutual connection and dependance, and to show how the operation of one event, or of one cause, prepared the way for another, and augmented its influence. We have hitherto been contemplating the progress of that darkness which spread over Europe from its first approach, to the period of greatest obscuration; a more pleasant exercise begins here, to observe the first dawnings of returning light, to mark the various accessions by which it gradually increased and advanced towards the full splendor of day.

I. The Crusades, or expeditions in order to rescue the Holy Land out of the hands of Infidels, seem to be the first event that rouzed Europe from the lethargy in which it had been long sunk, and that tended to introduce any change in government, or in manners. It is natural to the human mind to view those places which have been distinguished by being the residence of any illustrious personage, or the scene of any great transaction, with some degree of delight and veneration. From this principle flowed the superstitious devotion with which Christians, from the earliest ages of the church, were accustomed to visit that country which the Almighty had selected as the inheritance of his favourite people, and in which the son of God had accomplished the redemption of mankind. As this distant pilgrimage could not be performed without considerable expence, fatigue, and danger, it appeared the more meritorious, and came to be considered as an expiation for almost every crime. An opinion which spread with rapidity over Europe about the close of the tenth and beginning of the eleventh century, and which gained universal credit, wonderfully augmented the number of these credulous pilgrims, and increased the ardour with which they undertook this useless voyage. The thousand years mentioned by St. John[6] were supposed to be accomplished, and the end of the world to be at hand. A general consternation seized mankind; many relinquished their possessions; and abandoning their friends and families, hurried with precipitation to the Holy Land, where they imagined that Christ would quickly appear to judge the world.[7] While Palestine continued subject to the Caliphs, they had encouraged the resort of pilgrims to Jerusalem; and considered this as a beneficial species of commerce, which brought into their dominions gold and silver, and carried nothing out of them but relics and consecrated trinkets. But the Turks having conquered Syria about the middle of the eleventh century, pilgrims were exposed to outrages of every kind from these fierce barbarians. This change happening precisely at the juncture when the panic terror which I have mentioned rendered pilgrimages most frequent, filled Europe with alarm and indignation. Every person who returned from Palestine related the dangers which he had encountered, in visiting the holy city, and described with exaggeration the cruelty and vexations of the Turks.

When the minds of men were thus prepared, the zeal of a fanatical monk, who conceived the idea of leading all the forces of Christendom against the infidels, and of driving them out of the Holy Land by violence, was sufficient to give a beginning to that wild enterprize. Peter the hermit, for that was the name of this martial apostle, ran from province to province with a crucifix in his hand, exciting Princes and people to this Holy war, and wherever he came kindled the same enthusiastic ardour for it with which he himself was animated. The council of Placentia, where upwards of thirty thousand persons were assembled, pronounced the scheme to have been suggested by the immediate inspiration of heaven. In the council of Clermont, still more numerous, as soon as the measure was proposed, all cried out with one voice, "It is the will of God." Persons of all ranks were smitten with the contagion; not only the gallant nobles of that age, with their martial followers, whom the boldness of a romantic enterprize might have been apt to allure, but men in the more humble and pacific stations of life; ecclesiastics of every order, and even women and children engaged with emulation in an undertaking which was deemed sacred and meritorious. If we may believe the concurring testimony of contemporary authors, six millions of persons assumed the cross,[8] which was the badge that distinguished such as devoted themselves to this holy warfare. All Europe, says the Princess Anna Comnena, torn up from the foundation, seemed ready to precipitate itself in one united body upon Asia.[9] Nor did the fumes of this enthusiastic zeal evaporate at once: the frenzy was as lasting, as it was extravagant. During two centuries, Europe seems to have had no object but to recover, or keep possession of the Holy Land, and through that period, vast armies continued to march thither.

The first efforts of valour animated by enthusiasm were irresistible; part of the lesser Asia, all Syria and Palestine were wrested from the infidels; the banner of the cross was displayed on Mount Sion; Constantinople the capital of the Christian empire in the East, was seized by a body of these adventurers, who had taken arms against the Mahometans, and an Earl of Flanders, and his descendants, kept possession of the Imperial throne during half a century. But though the first impression of the Crusaders was so unexpected that they made their conquests with great ease, they found infinite difficulty in preserving them. Establishments so distant from Europe, surrounded by warlike nations, animated with fanatical zeal scarce inferior to that of the Crusaders themselves, were perpetually in danger of being overturned. Before the expiration of the thirteenth century, the Christians were driven out of all their Asiatic possessions, in acquiring of which incredible numbers of men had perished, and immense sums of money had been wasted. The only common enterprize in which

24

the European nations ever engaged, and which all undertook with equal ardour, remains a singular monument of human folly.

But from these expeditions, extravagant as they were, beneficial consequences followed, which had neither been foreseen nor expected. In their progress toward the Holy Land, the followers of the cross marched through countries better cultivated, and more civilized than their own. Their first rendezvous was commonly in Italy, in which Venice, Genoa, Pisa and other cities had begun to apply themselves to commerce, and had made some advances towards wealth as well as refinement. They embarked there, and landing in Dalmatia, pursued their route by land to Constantinople. Though the military spirit had been long extinct in the eastern Empire, and a despotism of the worst species had annihilated almost every publick virtue, yet Constantinople having never felt the destructive rage of the barbarous nations, was the greatest, as well as the most beautiful city in Europe, and the only one in which there remained any image of the ancient elegance in manners, and arts. The naval power of the eastern Empire was considerable. Manufactures of the most curious fabrick were carried on in its dominions. Constantinople was the only mart in Europe for the commodities of the East Indies. Although the Saracens and Turks had torn from the Empire many of its richest provinces, and had reduced it within very narrow bounds, yet great wealth flowed into the capital from these various sources, which not only cherished such a taste for magnificence but kept alive such a relish for the sciences as appear considerable when compared with what was known in other parts of Europe. Even in Asia, the Europeans who had assumed the cross found the remains of the knowledge and arts which the example and encouragement of the Caliphs had diffused through their empire. Although the attention of the historians of the Crusades was fixed on other objects than the state of society and manners among the nations which they invaded, although most of them had neither taste nor discernment enough to describe them, they relate, however, such signal acts of humanity and generosity in the conduct of Saladin as well as some other leaders of the Mahometans, as give us a very high idea of their manners. It was not possible for the Crusaders to travel through so many countries, and to behold their various customs and institutions without acquiring information and improvement. Their views enlarged; their prejudices wore off; new ideas crowded into their minds; and they must have been sensible on many occasions of the rusticity of their own manners when compared with those of a more polished people. These impressions were not so slight as to be effaced upon their return to their native countries. A close intercourse subsisted between the East and West during two centuries; new armies were continually marching from Europe to Asia, while former adventurers returned home and imported many of the customs to which they had been familiarized by a long residence abroad. Accordingly, we discover, soon after the commencement of the Crusades, greater splendour in the courts of Princes, greater pomp in publick ceremonies, a more refined taste in pleasure and amusements, together with a more romantic spirit of enterprize spreading gradually over Europe; and to these wild expeditions, the effect of superstition or folly, we owe the first gleams of light which tended to dispel barbarity and ignorance.

But these beneficial consequences of the Crusades took place slowly; their influence upon the state of property, and consequently of power, in the different kingdoms of Europe, was more immediate as well as discernible. The nobles who assumed the cross, and bound themselves to march to the Holy Land, soon perceived that great sums were necessary towards defraying the expences of such a distant expedition, and enabling them to appear with suitable dignity at the head of their vassals. But the genius of the feudal system was averse to the imposition of extraordinary taxes; and subjects in that age were unaccustomed to pay them. No expedient remained for levying the sums requisite, but the sale of their possessions. As men were inflamed with romantic expectations of the splendid conquests which they hoped to make in Asia, and possessed with such zeal for recovering the Holy Land as swallowed up every other passion, they relinquished their ancient inheritances without any reluctance, and for prices far below their value, that they might sally forth as adventurers in quest of new settlements in un-known countries. The Monarchs of the different kingdoms, none of whom had engaged in the first Crusade, eagerly seized this opportunity of annexing considerable territories to their crowns at small expense.[10] Besides this, several great barons who per-ished in the Holy war, having left no heirs, their fiefs reverted of course to their respective sovereigns, and by these accessions of property as well as power taken from the one scale and thrown into the other, the regal authority increased in proportion as that of the Aristocracy declined. The absence, too, of many potent vassals, accustomed to controul and give law to their sovereigns, afforded them an opportunity of extending their prerogative, and of acquiring a degree of weight in the constitution which they did not formerly possess. To these circumstances, we may add, that as all who assumed the cross, were taken under the immediate protection of the church, and its heaviest anathemas were de-nounced against such as should disquiet or annoy those who had devoted themselves to this service; the private quarrels and hos-tilities which banished tranquillity from a feudal kingdom were suspended or extinguished; a more general and steady admin-istration of justice began to be introduced, and some advances were made towards the establishment of regular government in the several kingdoms of Europe.[11]

The commercial effects of the Crusades were not less consid-erable than those which I have already mentioned. The first armies under the standard of the cross which Peter the hermit and Godfrey of Bouillon led through Germany and Hungary to Con-stantinople, suffered so much by the length of the march, as well as the fierceness of the barbarous people who inhabited those countries, that it deterred other from taking the same route; so that rather than encounter so many dangers, they chose to go by sea. Venice, Genoa, and Pisa furnished the transports on which they embarked. The sum which these cities received merely for freight from such numerous armies was immense.[12] This, how-ever, was but a small part of what they gained by the expeditions to the Holy Land; the Crusaders contracted with them, for mili-tary stores and provisions; their fleets kept on the coast as the army advanced by land; and supplying them with whatever was wanting, engrossed all the profits of that lucrative branch of commerce. The success which attended the arms of the Crusaders was productive of advantages still more permanent. There are charters yet extant, containing grants to the Venetians, Pisans, and Genoese of the most extensive immunities in the several settlements which the Christians made in Asia. All the commodities which they imported or exported are thereby exempted from every imposition; the property of entire suburbs in some of the maritime towns, and of large streets and houses in others, is vested in them; and all questions arising among persons settled within their precincts, or who traded under their protection, are appointed to be tried by their own laws and by judges of their own appointment.[13] When the Crusaders seized Constantinople, and placed one of their own number on the Imperial throne, the Italian States were likewise gainers by that event. The Venetians who had planned the enterprize, and took a considerable part in carrying it into execution, did not neglect to secure to themselves the chief advantages redounding from its success. They made themselves masters of part of the ancient Peloponnesus in Greece, together with some of the most fertile islands in the Archipelago. Many valuable branches of the commerce, which formerly centered in Constantinople, were transferred to Venice, Genoa, or Pisa. Thus a succession of events occasioned by the Holy War, opened various sources, from which wealth flowed in such abundance into these cities,[14] as enabled them, in concurrence with another institution which shall be immediately mentioned, to secure their own liberty and independance.

II. The institution to which I alluded was the forming of cities into communities, corporations, or bodies politick, and granting them the privilege of municipal jurisdiction, which contributed more, perhaps, than any other cause to introduce regular government, police and arts, and to diffuse them over Europe. The feudal government had degenerated into a system of oppression. The usurpations of the nobles were become unbounded and intolerable: they had reduced the great body of the people into a state of actual servitude: the condition of those dignified with the name of freemen, was often little preferable to that of the other. Nor was such oppression the portion of those alone who dwelt in the country, and were employed in cultivating the estate of their master. The cities and villages held of some great lord, on whom they depended for protection, and were no less subject to his arbitrary jurisdiction. The inhabitants were deprived of the natural, and most unalienable rights of humanity. They could not dispose of the effects whcih their own industry had acquired, either by a latter will, or by any deed executed during their life.[15] They had no right to appoint guardians for their children, during their minority. They were not permitted to marry without purchasing the consent of the lord on whom they depended.[16] If once they had commenced a law suit, they durst not terminate it by an accommodation, because that would have deprived the lord in whose court they pleaded, of the perquisites due to him on passing sentence.[17] Services of various kinds, no less disgraceful than oppressive, were exacted from them without mercy or moderation. The spirit of industry was choaked in some cities by absurd regulations, and in others by unreasonable exactions: nor would the narrow and oppressive maxims of a military aristocracy have permitted it ever to rise to any degree of height or vigour.[18]

But as soon as the cities of Italy began to turn their attention towards commerce, and to conceive some idea of the advantages which they might derive from it, they became impatient to shake off the yoke of their insolent lords, and to establish among themselves such a free and equal government as would render property secure, and industry flourishing. The German Emperors, especially those of the Franconian and Suabian lines, as the seat of their government was far distant from Italy, possessed a feeble and imperfect jurisdiction in that country. Their perpetual quarrels either with the Popes or with their own turbulent vassals diverted their attention from the interior police of Italy, and gave constant employment to their arms. These circumstances encouraged the inhabitants of some of the Italian cities, towards the beginning of the eleventh century, to assume new privileges, to unite together more closely, and to form themselves into bodies politick governed by laws established by common consent.[19] The rights, which many cities acquired by bold or fortunate usurpations, others purchased from the Emperors, who deemed themselves gainers when they received large sums for immunities which they were no longer able to withhold; and some cities obtained them gratuitously from the generosity or facility of the Princes on whom they depended. The great increase of wealth which the Crusades brought into Italy, occasioned a new kind of fermentation and activity in the minds of the people, and excited such a general passion for liberty and independance, that before the conclusion of the last Crusade all the considerable cities in that country had either purchased or had extorted large immunities from the Emperors.

This innovation was not long known in Italy before it made its way into France. Louis the Gross, in order to create some power that might counterbalance those potent vassals who controuled, or gave law to the crown, first adopted the plan of conferring new privileges on the towns situated within his own domaine. These privileges were called *charter of community,* by which he enfranchised the inhabitants, abolished all marks of servitude, and formed them into corporations or bodies politick, to be governed by a council and magistrates of their own nomination. These magistrates had the right of administring justice within their own precincts, of levying taxes, of embodying and training to arms the militia of the town, which took the field when required by the sovereign, under the command of officers appointed by the community. The great barons imitated the example of their monarch, and grant like immunities to the towns within their territories. They had wasted such great sums in their expeditions to the Holy Land, that they were eager to lay hold on this new expedient for raising money, by the sale of these charters of liberty. Though the institution of communities was as repugnant to their maxims of policy, as it was adverse to their power, they disregarded remote consequences, in order to obtain present relief. In less than two centuries servitude was abolished in most of the towns in France, and they became free corporations, instead of dependant villages without jurisdiction or privileges. Much about the same period, the great cities in Germany began to acquire like immunities, and laid the foundation of their present liberty and independance. The practice spread quickly over Europe, and was adopted in Germany, Spain, England, Scotland, and all the other feudal kingdoms.

The good effects of this new institution were immediately felt, and its influence on government as well as manners was no less extensive than salutary. A great body of the people was released from servitude, and from all the arbitrary and grievous impositions to which that wretched condition had subjected them. Towns, upon acquiring the right of community, became so many little republicks, governed by known and equal laws; and liberty was deemed such an essential and characteristic part in their constitution, that if any slave took refuge in one of them, and resided there during a year without being claimed, he was instantly declared a freeman, and admitted as a member of the community.[20]

As one part of the people owed their liberty to the erection of communities, another was indebted to them for their security. Such has been the state of Europe during several centuries, that self-preservation obliged every man to court the patronage of some powerful baron, and in times of danger his castle was the place to which all resorted for safety. But towns surrounded with walls, whose inhabitants were regularly trained to arms, and bound by interest, as well as by the most solemn engagements, reciprocally to defend each other, afforded a more commodious and secure retreat. The nobles began to be considered as of less importance, when they ceased to be the sole guardians to whom the people could look up for protection against violence.

If the nobility suffered some diminution of their credit and power by the privileges granted to the cities, the crown acquired an increase of both. As there were no regular troops kept on foot in any of the feudal kingdoms, the Monarch could bring no army into the field but what was composed of soldiers furnished by the crown-vassals, always jealous of the regal authority, and often in rebellion against it; nor had he any funds for carrying on the publick service, but such as they granted him with a very sparing

31

hand. But when the members of communities were permitted to bear arms, and were trained to the use of these, this in some degree supplied the first defect, and gave the crown the command of a body of men independant of its great vassals. The attachment of the cities to their sovereigns, whom they respected as the first authors of their liberties, and whom they were obliged to court as the protectors of their immunities against the domineering spirit of the nobles, contributed somewhat towards removing the second evil, as it frequently engaged them to grant the crown such supplies of money as added new force to government.[21]

The acquisition of liberty made such a happy change in the condition of all members of communities, as roused them from that stupidity and inaction into which they had been sunk by the wretchedness of their former state. The spirit of industry revived. Commerce became an object of attention, and began to flourish. Population increased. Independance was established; and wealth flowed into cities which had long been the seat of poverty and oppression. Wealth was accompanied by its usual attendants, ostentation and luxury; and though the former was inelegant and cumbersome, and the latter indelicate, they led gradually to greater refinements in manners, and in the habits of life. Together with this improvement in manners, a more regular species of government and police was introduced. As cities grew to be more populous, and the occasions of intercourse among men increased, statutes and regulations multiplied of course, and all became sensible that their common safety depended on observing them with exactness, and on punishing such as violated them, with promptitude and rigour. Laws and subordination, as well as polished manners, took their rise in cities, and diffused themselves insensibly through the rest of the society.

III. The inhabitants of cities having obtained personal freedom and municipal jurisdiction, soon acquired civil liberty and political power. It was a fundamental principle in the feudal system of policy, that no freeman could be governed or taxed unless by his own consent. In consequence of this, the vassals of every baron were called to his court, in which they established by mutual consent such regulations as they deemed most beneficial to their small society, and granted their superior such supplies of money as were proportional to their abilities, or to his wants. The barons themselves, conformably to the same maxim, were admitted into the supreme assembly of the nation, and concurred with the sovereign in enacting laws, or in imposing taxes. As the superior lord, according to the original plan of feudal policy, retained the direct property of those lands which he granted, in temporary possession, to his vassals, the law, even after fiefs became hereditary, still supposed this original practice to subsist, and a baron continued to be considered as the guardian of all who resided within his territories. The great council of each nation, whether distinguished by the name of a parliament, a diet, the Cortes, or the states general, was composed entirely of such barons, and dignified ecclesiasticks, as held immediately of the the crown. Towns, whether situated within the royal domaine, or on the lands of a subject, depended for protection on the lord of whom they held. They had no legal name, no political existence, which could entitle them to be admitted into the legislative assembly, or could give them any authority there. But as soon as they were enfranchised, and formed into Bodies Corporate, they became legal and independant members of the constitution, and acquired all the rights essential to freemen. Amongst these, the most valuable, was the privilege of a decisive voice in enacting laws, and in granting subsidies. It was natural for cities, accustomed to a form of municipal government, according to which no regulation could be established, and no money could be raised without their own consent, to claim this privilege. The wealth, the power and consideration which they acquired on recovering their liberty added weight to their claim; and favourable events happened, or fortunate conjunctures occurred in the different kingdoms of Europe, which facilitated or forwarded their obtaining possession of this important right. In England, one of the first countries in which the representatives of boroughs were admitted into the great council of the nation, the barons who took arms against Henry III summoned them to attend parliament in order to add greater popularity to their party, and to strengthen the barrier against the encroachment of regal power. In France, Philip the Fair, a Monarch no less sagacious than enterprizing, considered them as instruments which might be employed with equal advantage to extend the royal prerogative, to counterbalance the exorbitant power of the nobles, and to facilitate the imposition of new taxes. With these views, he introduced the deputies of such towns as were formed into communities into the states general of the nation.[22] In the Empire, the wealth and immunities of the Imperial cities placed them on a level with the most considerable members of the Germanic body. Conscious of their own power and dignity, they pretended to the privilege of forming a separate bench in the diet; and made good their pretension.[23]

But in what way soever the representatives of cities first gained a place in the legislature, that even had great influence on the form and genius of government. It tempered the rigour of aristocratical oppression, with a proper mixture of popular liberty: It secured to the great body of the people, who had formerly no representatives, active and powerful guardians of their rights and privileges: It established an intermediate power between the King and nobles, to which each had recourse alternately, and which at some times opposed the usurpations of the former, on other occasions checked the encroachments of the latter. As soon as the representatives of communities gained any degree of credit and influence in the legislature, the spirit of laws became different from what it had formerly been; it flowed from new principles; it was directed towards new objects; equality, order, the publick good, and the redress of grievances, were phrases and ideas brought into use, and which grew to be familiar in the statutes and jurisprudence of the European nations. Almost all the efforts in favour of liberty in every country of Europe have been made by this new power in the legislature. In proportion as it rose to consideration and influence, the severity of the aristocratical spirit decreased; and the privileges of the people became gradually more extensive as the ancient and exorbitant jurisdiction of the nobles was abridged.

IV. The inhabitants of towns having been declared free by the charters of communities, that part of the people which resided in the country, and was employed in agriculture, began to recover liberty by enfranchisement. During the rigour of feudal government, as hath been already observed, the great body of the lower people was reduced to servitude. They were slaves fixed to the soil which they cultivated, and together with it were transferred from one proprietor to another, by sale, or by conveyance. The spirit of feudal policy did not favour the enfranchisement of that order of men. It was an established maxim that no vassal could legally diminish the value of a fief, to the detriment of the lord from whom he had received it. In consequence of this, manumission by the authority of the immediate master was not valid; and unless it was confirmed by the superior lord of whom he held, slaves of this species did not acquire a compleat right to their liberty. Thus it became necessary to ascend through all the gradations of feudal holding to the King, the lord Paramount.[24] A form of procedure so tedious and troublesome discouraged the practice of manumission. Domestic or personal slaves often obtained liberty from the humanity or beneficence of their masters, to whom they belonged in absolute property. The condition of slaves fixed to the soil was much more unalterable.

But the freedom and independence which one part of the people had obtained by the institution of communities, inspired the other with the most ardent desire of acquiring the same privileges; and their superiors, sensible of the benefits which they themselves had derived from former concessions, were less unwilling to gratify them by the grant of new immunities. The enfranchisement of slaves became more frequent; and the Monarchs of France, prompted by necessity, no less than by their inclination to reduce the power of the nobles, endeavoured to render it general. Louis X and his brother Philip issued ordinances, declaring, "That as all men were by nature freeborn, and as their kingdom was called the kingdom of Franks, they determined that it should be so in reality as well as in name; therefore they appointed that enfranchisements should be granted throughout the whole kingdom, upon just and reasonable conditions."[25] These edicts were carried into immediate execution within the royal domaine. The example of their sovereigns, together with the expectation of the considerable sums which they might raise by this expedient, led many of the nobles to set their dependants at liberty; and servitude was gradually abolished in almost every province of the kingdom. In Italy, the establishment of republican government in their great cities, the genius and maxims of which were extremely different from those of the feudal policy, together with the ideas of equality which the progress of commerce had rendered familiar, gradually introduced the practice of enfranchising the ancient *predial* slaves. In some provinces of Germany, the persons who had been subject to this species of bondage, were released; in others, the rigour of their state was mitigated. In England, as the spirit of liberty gained ground, the very name and idea of personal servitude, without any formal interposition of the legislature to prohibit it, was totally banished.

The effects of such a remarkable change in the condition of so great a part of the people, could not fail of being considerable and extensive. The husbandman, master of his own industry, and secure of reaping for himself the fruits of his labour, became the farmer of the same fields where he had formerly been compelled to toil for the benefit of another. The odious names of master and of slave, the most mortifying and depressing of all distinctions to human nature, were abolished. New prospects opened, and new incitements to ingenuity and enterprize presented themselves, to those who were emancipated. The expectation of bettering their fortune, as well as that of raising themselves to a more honourable condition, concurred in calling forth their activity and genius; and a numerous class of men, who formerly had no political existence, and were employed merely as instruments of labour, became useful citizens, and contributed towards augmenting the force or riches of the society, which adopted them as members.

V. The various expedients which were employed in order to introduce a more regular, equal, and vigorous administration of justice, contributed greatly towards the improvement of society. What was the particular mode of dispensing justice in the several barbarous nations which over-ran the Roman Empire, and took possession of its different provinces, cannot now be determined with certainty. We may conclude from the form of government established among them, as well as from their ideas concerning the nature of society, that the authority of the magistrate was extremely limited, and the independance of individuals proportionally great. History and records, as far as they reach back, justify this conclusion, and represent the ideas and exercise of justice in all the countries of Europe, as little different from those which must take place in a state of nature. To maintain the order and tranquillity of society by the regular execution of known laws; to inflict vengeance on crimes destructive of the peace and safety of individuals, by a prosecution carried on in the name, and by the authority of the community; to consider the punishment of criminals as a public example to deter others from violating the laws; were objects of government little understood in theory, and less regarded in practice. The magistrate could scarce be said to hold the sword of justice; it was left in the hands of private persons. Resentment was almost the sole motive for prosecuting crimes; and to gratify that passion, was the end and rule in punishing them. He who suffered the wrong, was the only person who had a right to pursue the aggressor, and to exact or to remit the punishment. From a system of judicial procedure, so crude and defective as seems to be scarce compatible with the subsistence of civil society, disorder and anarchy flowed. Superstition concurred with this ignorance concerning the nature of government, in obstructing the administration of justice, or in rendering it capricious and unequal. To provide remedies for these evils, so as to give a more regular course to justice, was, during several centuries, one great object of political wisdom. The regulations for this purpose, may be reduced to three general heads: To explain these, and to point out the manner in which they operated is an important article in the history of society among the nations of Europe.

1. The first considerable step towards establishing an equal administration of justice, was the abolishment of the right which individuals claimed of waging war with each other, in their own name, and by their own authority. To repel injuries, and

to revenge wrongs, is no less natural to man than to cultivate friendship; and while society remains in its most simple state, the former is considered as a personal right no less unalienable than the latter. Nor do men in this situation deem that they have a title to redress their own wrongs alone; they are touched with the injuries of those with whom they are connected, or in whose honour they are interested; and are no less prompt to avenge them. The savage, how imperfectly soever he may comprehend the principles of political union, feels warmly the sentiments of social affection, and the obligations arising from the ties of blood. On the appearance of an injury or affront offered to his family or tribe, he kindles into rage, and pursues the authors of it with the keenest resentment. He considers it as cowardly to expect redress from any arm but his own, and as infamous to give up to another the right of determining what reparation he should accept, or with what vengeance he should rest satisfied.

The maxims and practice of all uncivilized nations, with respect to the prosecution and punishment of offenders, particularly those of the ancient Germans, and other Barbarians who invaded the Roman Empire, are perfectly conformable to these ideas.[26] While they retained their native simplicity of manners, and continued to be divided into small tribes or societies, the defects in this imperfect system of criminal jurisprudence, (if it merits that name) were less sensibly felt. When they came to settle in the extensive provinces which they had conquered, and to form themselves into great monarchies; when new objects of ambition presenting themselves, increased both the number and the violence of their dissensions, they ought to have adopted new maxims concerning the redress of injuries, and to have regulated by general and equal laws, that which they formerly left to be directed by the caprice of private passion. But fierce and haughty chieftains, accustomed to avenge themselves on such as had injured them, did not think of relinquishing a right which they considered as a privilege of their order, and a mark of their independance. Laws enforced by the authority of Princes and Magistrates who possessed little power, commanded no great degree of reverence. The administration of justice among rude illiterate people, was not so accurate or decisive, or uniform, as to induce men to submit implicitly to its determinations. Every offended baron buckled on his armour, and sought redress at the head of his vassals. His adversary met him in like hostile array. Neither of them appealed to impotent laws which could afford them no protection. Neither of them would submit points, in which their passions were warmly interested, to the slow determination of a judicial enquiry. Both trusted to their swords for the decision of the contest. The kindred and dependants of the aggressor, as well as of the defender, were involved in the quarrel. They had not even the liberty of remaining neutral. Such as refused to act in concert with the party to which they belonged, were not only exposed to infamy, but subjected to legal penalties.

The different kingdoms of Europe were torn and afflicted, during several centuries, by intestine wars, excited by private animosities, and carried on with all the rage natural to men of fierce manners, and of violent passions. The estate of every baron was a kind of independant territory, disjoined from those around it, and the hostilities between them were perpetual. The evil became so inveterate and deep-rooted, that the form and laws of private war were ascertained, and regulations concerning it made a part in the system of jurisprudence,[27] in the same manner as if this practice had been founded in some natural right of humanity, or in the original constitution of civil society.

So great was the disorder, and such the calamities which these perpetual hostilities occasioned, that various efforts were made to wrest from the nobles this pernicious privilege which they claimed. It was the interest of every sovereign to abolish a practice which almost annihilated his authority. Charlemagne prohibited it by an express law, as an invention of the devil to destroy the order and happiness of society;[28] but the reign of one Monarch, however vigorous and active, was too short to extirpate a custom so firmly established. Instead of enforcing this prohibition, his feeble successors durst venture on nothing more than to apply palliatives. They declared it unlawful for any person to commence war, until he had sent a formal defiance to the kindred and dependants of his adversary; they ordained that, after the commission of the trespass or crime which gave rise to a private war, forty days must elapse before the person injured should attack the vassals of his adversary; they enjoined all persons to suspend their private animosities, and to cease from hostilities when the King was engaged in any war against the enemies of the nation. The church co-operated with the civil magistrate, and interposed its authority in order to extirpate a practice so repugnant to the spirit of Christianity. Various councils issued decrees, prohibiting all private wars; and denounced the heaviest anathemas against such as should disturb the tranquillity of society, by claiming or exercising that barbarous right. The aid of religion was called in to combat and subdue the ferocity of the times. The Almighty was said to have manifested, by visions and revelations to different persons, his disapprobation of that spirit of revenge, which armed one part of his creatures against the other. Men were required, in the name of God, to sheath their swords, and to remember the sacred ties which united them as Christians, and as members of the same society. But this junction of civil and ecclesiastic authority, though strengthened by every thing most apt to alarm and over-awe the credulous spirit of those ages, produced no other effect than some temporary suspensions of hostilities, and a cessation from war on certain days and seasons consecrated to the more solemn acts of devotion. The nobles continued to assert this dangerous privilege; they refused to obey some of the laws calculated to annul or circumscribe it; they eluded others; they petitioned; they remonstrated; they struggled for the right of private war as the highest and most honourable distinction of their order. Even so late as the fourteenth century, we find the nobles in several provinces of France contending for their ancient method of terminating their differences by the sword, in preference to that of submitting them to the decision of any judge. The final abolition of this practice in that kingdom, and the other countries in which it prevailed, is not to be ascribed so much to the force of statutes and decrees, as to the gradual increase of the royal authority, and to the imperceptible progress of juster sentiments concerning government, order, and public security.

2. The prohibition of the form of trial by judicial combat, was another considerable step towards the introduction of such regular government as secured publick order and private tranquillity. As the right of private war left many of the quarrels among individuals to be decided, like those between nations, by arms; the form of trial by judicial combat, which was established in every country in Europe, banished equity from courts of justice, and rendered chance or force the arbiter of their determinations. In civilized nations, all transactions of any importance are concluded in writing. The exhibition of the deed or instrument is full evidence of the fact, and ascertains with precision what each party has stipulated to perform. But among a rude people, when the arts of reading and writing were such uncommon attainments, that to be master of either, intitled a person to the appellation of a clerk or learned man, scarce any thing was committed to writing but treaties between Princes, their grants and charters to their subjects, or such transactions between private parties as were of extraordinary consequence, or had an extensive effect. The greater part of affairs in common life and business were carried on by verbal contracts or promises. This, in many civil questions, not only made it difficult to bring proof sufficient to establish any claim, but encouraged falsehood and fraud, by rendering them extremely easy. Even in criminal cases, where a particular fact must be ascertained, or an accusation be disproved, the nature and effect of legal evidence was little understood by barbarous nations. To define with accuracy that species of evidence which a court had reason to expect; to determine when it ought to insist on positive proof, and when it should be satisfied with a proof from circumstances; to compare the testimony of discordant witnesses; and to fix the degree of credit due to each; were discussions too intricate and subtile for the jurisprudence of ignorant ages. In order to avoid encumbering themselves with these, a more simple form of procedure was introduced into courts as well civil as criminal. In all cases, where the notoriety of the

fact did not furnish the clearest and most direct evidence, the person accused, or he against whom an action was brought, was called legally, or offered voluntarily to purge himself by oath; and upon his declaring his innocence, he was instantly acquitted.[29] This absurd practice effectually screened guilt and fraud from detection or punishment, by rendering the temptation to perjury so powerful, that it was not easy to resist it. The pernicious effects of it were sensibly felt; and in order to guard against them, the laws ordained that oaths should be administered with great solemnity, and accompanied with every circumstance which could inspire religious reverence, or superstitious terror.[30] This, however, proved a feeble remedy: these ceremonious rites became familiar, and their impression on the imagination gradually diminished; men who could venture to disregard truth, were not apt to startle at the solemnities of an oath. Their observation of this, put legislators upon devising a new expedient for rendering the purgation by oath more certain and satisfactory. They required the person accused to appear with a certain number of freemen, his neighbours or relations, who corroborated the oath which he took, by swearing that they believed all that he had uttered to be true. These were called *Compurgators,* and their number varied according to the importance of the subject in dispute, or the nature of the crime with which a person was charged.[31] In some cases, the concurrence of no less than three hundred of these auxiliary witnesses was requisite to acquit the person accused.[32] But even this device was found to be ineffectual. It was a point of honour with every man in Europe, during several ages, not to desert the chief on whom he depended, and to stand by those with whom the ties of blood connected him. Whoever then was bold enough to violate the laws, was sure of devoted adherents, willing to abet, and eager to serve him in whatever manner he required. The formality of calling Compurgators, proved an apparent, not a real security, against falsehood and perjury; and the sentences of courts, while they continued to refer every point in question to the oath of the defendant, became so flagrantly iniquitous as excited universal indignation against this method of procedure.[33]

Sensible of these defects, but strangers to the manner of correcting them, or of introducing a more proper form, our ancestors, as an infallible method of discovering truth, and of guarding against deception, appealed to Heaven, and referred every point in dispute to be determined, as they imagined, by the decisions of unerring wisdom and impartial justice. The person accused, in order to prove his innocence, submitted, in some cases, to trial, by plunging his arm in boiling water; by lifting a red-hot iron with his naked hand; by walking bare-foot over burning plough-shares; or by other experiments equally perilous and formidable. On other occasions, he challenged his accuser to fight him in single combat. All these various forms of trial were conducted with many devout ceremonies; the ministers of religion were employed, the Almighty was called upon to interpose for the manifestation of guilt, and for the protection of innocence; and who ever escaped unhurt, or came off victorious, was pronounced to be acquitted by the *Judgment of God*.[34]

Among all the whimsical and absurd institutions which owe their existence to the weakness of human reason, this, which submitted questions that affected the property, the reputation, and the lives of men, to the determination of chance, or of bodily strength and address, appears to be the most extravagant and preposterous. There were circumstances, however, which led the nations of Europe to consider this equivocal mode of deciding any point in contest, as a direct appeal to heaven, and a certain method of discovering its will. As men are unable to comprehend the manner in which the Almighty carries on the government of the universe, by equal, fixed, and general laws, they are apt to imagine that in every case which their passions or interest render important in their own eyes, the Supreme Ruler of all ought visibly to display his power, in vindicating innocence and punishing vice. It requires no inconsiderable degree of science and philosophy to correct this popular error. But the sentiments prevalent in Europe during the dark ages, instead of correcting, strengthened it. Religion, for several centuries, consisted chiefly in believing the legendary history of those saints whose names crowd and disgrace the Romish calendar. The fabulous tales concerning their miracles, had been declared authentic by the bulls of Popes, and the decrees of councils; they made the great subject of the instructions which the clergy offered to the people, and were received by them with implicit credulity and admiration. By these, men were accustomed to believe that the established laws of nature might be violated on the most frivolous occasions, and were taught to look rather for particular and extraordinary acts of power under the divine administration, than to contemplate the regular progress and execution of a general plan. One superstition prepared the way for another; and whoever believed that the Supreme Being had interposed miraculously on those trivial occasions mentioned in legends, could not but expect his intervention in matters of greater importance, when solemnly referred to his decision.

With this superstitious opinion, the martial spirit of Europe, during the middle ages, concurred in establishing the mode of trial by judicial combat. To be ready to maintain with his sword whatever his lips had uttered, was the first maxim of honour with every gentleman. To assert their own rights by force of arms, to inflict vengeance on those who had injured or affronted them, were the distinction and pride of high-spirited nobles. The form of trial by combat coinciding with this maxim, flattered and gratified these passions. Every man was the guardian of his own honour, and of his own life; the justice of his cause, as well as his future reputation, depended on his own courage and prowess. This mode of decision was considered, accordingly, as one of the happiest efforts of wise policy; and as soon as it was introduced, all the forms of trial by fire or water, and other superstitious experiments, fell into disuse, or were employed only in controversies between persons of inferior rank. The trial by combat was authorized over all Europe, and received in every country with equal satisfaction. Not only questions concerning uncertain or contested facts, but general and abstract points in law were determined by the issue of a combat; and the latter was deemed a method of discovering truth more liberal as well as more satisfactory, than that by examination and argument. Not only might parties, whose minds were exasperated by the eagerness and the hostility of opposition, defy their antagonist, and require him to make good his charge, or to prove his innocence, with his sword; but witnesses, who had no interest in the issue of the question, though called to declare the truth by laws which ought to have afforded them protection, were equally exposed to the danger of a challenge, and equally bound to assert the veracity of their evidence by dint of arms. To complete the absurdities of this military jurisprudence, even the character of a judge was not sacred from its violence. Any one of the parties might interrupt a judge when about to deliver his opinion; might accuse him of iniquity and corruption in the most reproachful terms, and throwing down his gauntlet, might challenge him to defend his integrity in the field; nor could he, without infamy, refuse to accept the defiance, or decline to enter the lists against such an adversary.

Thus the form of trial by combat, like other abuses, spread gradually, and extended to all persons and almost to all cases. Ecclesiastics, women, minors, superannuated and infirm persons, who could not with decency or justice be compelled to take arms, and to maintain their own cause, were obliged to produce champions, whom they engaged by affection or rewards, to fight their battles. The solemnities of a judicial combat were such as were natural in an action, which was considered both as a formal appeal to God, and as the final decision of questions of the highest moment. Every circumstance relating to them was regulated by the edicts of Princes, and explained in the comments of lawyers, with a minute and even superstitious accuracy. Skill in these laws and rites was the only science of which warlike nobles boasted, or which they were ambitious to attain.[35]

By this barbarous custom the natural course of proceeding, both in civil and criminal questions, was entirely perverted. Force usurped the place of equity in courts of judicature, and justice was banished from her proper mansion. Discernment, learning, integrity, were qualities less necessary to a judge than bodily strength, and dexterity in the use of arms. Daring courage, and superior vigour or address, were of more moment towards securing the favourable issue of a suit, than the equity of a cause, or the clearness of the evidence. Men, of course, applied them-selves to cultivate the talents which they found to be of greatest utility. As strength of body and address in arms were no less requisite in those lists which they were obliged to enter in defence of their private rights, than in the field of battle, where they met the enemies of their country, the great object of education, it became the chief employment in life, as well as to acquire these martial accomplishments. The administration of justice, instead of accustoming men to listen to the voice of equity, or to reverence the decisions of law, added to the ferocity of their manners, and taught them to consider force as the great arbiter of right and wrong.

These pernicious effects of the trial by combat were so ob-vious, that they did not altogther escape the view of the un-observing age in which it was introduced. The clergy, from the beginning, remonstrated against it as repugnant to the spirit of Christianity, and subversive of justice and order.[36] But the maxims and passions which favoured it, had taken such hold of the minds of men, that they disregarded admonitions and cen-sures, which, on other occasions, would have struck them with terror. The evil was too great and inveterate to yield to that remedy, and continuing to increase, the civil power at length found it necessary to interpose. Conscious, however, of their own limited authority, monarchs proceeded with caution, and their first attempts to restrain, or to set any bounds to this practice, were extremely feeble. One of the earliest restrictions of this practice which occurs in the history of Europe, is that of Henry I of England. It extended no farther than to prohibit the trial by combat in questions concerning property of small value.[37] Louis VII of France imitated his example, and issued an edict to the same effect.[38] St. Louis, whose ideas as a legislator, were far superior to those of his age, endeavoured to introduce a more perfect jurisprudence, and to substitute the trial by evidence, in place of that by combat. But his regulations, with respect to this, were confined to his own domains; for the great vassals of the crown, possessed such independant authority, and were so fondly attached to the ancient practice, that he durst not venture to extend it to the whole kingdom. Some barons voluntarily adopted his regulations. The spirit of courts of justice became averse to the mode of decision by combat, and discouraged it on every occasion. The nobles, nevertheless, thought it so honourable to depend for the security of their lives and fortunes on their own courage alone, and contended with so much vehemence for the preservation of this favourite privilege of their order, that the successors of St. Louis, unable to oppose, and afraid of offending such powerful subjects, were obliged not only to tolerate, but to authorize the practice which he had attempted to abolish.[39] In other countries of Europe, efforts equally zealous were employed to maintain the established custom; and similar concessions were extorted from their respective sovereigns. It continued, however, to be an object of policy with every monarch of abilities or vigour, to explode the trial by combat; and various edicts were issued for this purpose. But the observation which was made concerning the right of private war, is equally applicable to the mode of trial under review. No custom, how absurd soever it may be, if it has subsisted long, or derives its force from the manners and prejudices of the age in which it prevails, was ever abolished by the bare promulgation of laws and statutes. The sentiments of the people must change, or some new power sufficient to counteract it must be introduced. Such a change, accordingly, took place in Europe, as science gradually increased, and society advanced towards more perfect order. In proportion as the prerogative of Princes extended, and came to acquire new force, a power, interested in suppressing every practice favourable to the independance of the nobles, was introduced. The struggle, nevertheless, subsisted for several centuries; sometimes the new regulations and ideas seemed to gain ground; sometimes ancient habits recurred; and though, upon the whole, the trial by combat went more and more into disuse, yet instances of it occur, as late as the sixteenth century, in the history both of France and England. In proportion as it declined, the regular administration of justice was restored, the proceedings of courts were directed by known laws, the study of these became an object of attention to judges, and the people of Europe advanced fast towards civility, when this great cause of the ferocity of their manners was removed.

3. By authorizing the right of appeal from the courts of the Barons to those of the King, and subjecting the decisions of the former to the review of the latter, a new step, not less considerable that these which I have already mentioned, was taken towards establishing the regular, consistent, and vigorous administration of justice. Among all the encroachments of the feudal nobles on the prerogative of their Monarchs, their usurping the administration of justice with supreme authority, both in civil and criminal causes, within the precincts of their own estates, was the most singular. In other nations, subjects have contended with their Princes, and have endeavoured to extend their own power and privileges; but in the history of their struggles and pretensions, we discover nothing similar to this right which the feudal barons claimed, and acquired. It must have been something peculiar in their genius and manners that suggested this idea, and prompted them to insist on such a claim. Among the rude people who conquered the various provinces of the Roman Empire, and established new kingdoms there, the passion of resentment, too impetuous to bear controul, was permitted to remain almost unrestrained by the authority of laws. The person offended, as has been observed, retained not only the right of prosecuting but of punishing his adversary. To him it belonged to inflict such vengeance as satiated his rage, or to accept of such satisfaction as appeased it. But while fierce barbarians continued to be the sole judges in their own cause, their enmities were implacable, and immortal; they set no bounds either to the degree of their vengeance, or to the duration of their resentment. The excesses which this occasioned, proved so destructive of peace and order in society, as forced them to think of some remedy. At first, arbiters interposed, and by persuasion or intreaty prevailed on the party offended to accept of a fine or composition from the aggressor, and to drop all farther prosecution. But as submission to persons who had no legal or magisterial authority, was altogether voluntary, it became necessary to establish judges with power sufficient to enforce their own decisions. The leader whom

they were accustomed to follow and to obey, whose courage they respected, and in whose integrity they placed confidence, was the person to whom a martial people naturally committed this important prerogative. Every chieftain was the commander of his tribe in war, and their judge in peace. Every baron led his vassals to the field, and administered justice to them in his hall. Their high-spirited dependants would not have recognized any other authority, or have submitted to any other jurisdiction. But in times of turbulence and violence, the exercise of this new function was attended not only with trouble, but with danger. No person could assume the character of a judge, if he did not possess power sufficient to protect the one party from the violence of private revenge, and to compel the other to accept of such reparation as he enjoined. In consideration of the extraordinary efforts which this office required, judges, besides the fine which they appointed to be paid as a compensation to the person or family who had been injured, levied an additional sum as a recompence for their own labour; and in all the feudal kingdoms the latter was as precisely ascertained, and as regularly exacted, as the former.

Thus, by the natural operation of circumstances peculiar to the manners or political state of the feudal nations, separate and territorial jurisdictions came not only to be established in every kingdom, but were established in such a way, that the interest of the barons concurred with their ambition in maintaining and extending them. It was not merely a point of honour with the feudal nobles to dispense justice to their vassals; but from the exercise of that power arose one capital branch of their revenue; and the emoluments of their courts were frequently the main support of their dignity. It was with infinite zeal that they asserted and defended this high privilege of their order. By this institution, however, every kingdom in Europe was split into as many separate principalities as it contained powerful barons. Their vassals, whether in peace or in war, were scarce sensible of any authority, but that of their superior lord. They felt themselves subject to no other command. They were amenable to no other jurisdiction. The ties which linked together these smaller confederacies became close and firm; the bonds of public union relaxed, or were dissolved. The nobles strained their invention in devising regulations that tended to ascertain and perpetuate this distinction. In order to guard against any appearance of subordination in their courts to those of the crown, they constrained their monarchs to prohibit the royal judges from entering their territories, or from claiming any jurisdiction there; and if, either through mistake, or from the spirit of encroachment, any royal judge ventured to extend his authority to the vassals of a baron, they might plead their right of exemption, and the lord of whom they held could not only rescue them out of his hands, but was entitled to legal reparation for the injury and affront offered to him. The jurisdiction of the royal judges scarce reached beyond the narrow limits of the King's demesnes. Instead of a regular gradation of courts, all acknowledging the authority of the same general laws, and looking up to these as the guides of their decisions, there were in every feudal kingdom a thousand independant tribunals, the proceedings of which were directed by local customs and contradictory forms. The collision of jurisdiction between these numerous courts, often retarded the execution of justice: The variety and caprice of their modes of procedure must have for ever kept the administration of it from attaining any degree of uniformity or perfection.

All the monarchs of Europe perceived these encroachments on their jurisdiction, and bore them with impatience. But the usurpations of the nobles were so firmly established, and the danger of endeavouring to overturn them by open force was so manifest, that they were obliged to remain satisfied with attempts to undermine them. Various expedients were employed for this purpose; each of which merit attention, as they mark the progress of law and equity in the several kingdoms of Europe. At first, Princes endeavoured to circumscribe the jurisdiction of the barons, by permitting them to take cognizance only of smaller offences, reserving those of greater moment, under the appellation of *Pleas of the Crown,* and *Royal Causes,* to be tried in the King's courts. This affected only the barons of inferior note; the more powerful nobles scorned such a distinction, and not only claimed unlimited jurisdiction, but obliged their sovereigns to grant them charters, conveying or recognizing this privilege in the most ample form. The attempt, nevertheless, was productive of some good consequences, and paved the way for more. It turned the attention of men towards a jurisdiction distinct from that of the baron whose vassals they were; it accustomed them to the pretensions of superiority which the crown claimed over territorial judges; and taught them, when oppressed by their own superior lords, to look up to their sovereign as their protector. This facilitated the introduction of appeals, by which Princes brought the decisions of the baron's courts under the review of the royal judges. While trial by combat subsisted in full vigour, no point decided according to that mode, could be brought under the review of another court. It had been referred to the judgment of God; the issue of battle had declared his will; and it would have been impious to have called in question the equity of the divine decision. But as soon as that barbarous custom began to fall into disuse, Princes encouraged the vassals of the baron to sue for redress, by appealing to the royal courts. The progress, however, of this practice, was slow and gradual. The first instances of appeal were on account of *the delay* or *the refusal of justice* in the baron's court; and as these were countenanced by the ideas of subordination in the feudal constitution, the nobles allowed them to be introduced without much opposition. But when these were followed by appeals on account of *the injustice* or *iniquity of the sentence,* the nobles then began to be sensible, that if this innovation became general, the shadow of power alone would remain in their hands, and all real authority and jurisdiction would center in those courts which possessed the right of review. They instantly took the alarm, remonstrated against the encroachment, and contended boldly for their ancient privileges. But the monarchs in the different kingdoms of Europe pursued their plan with steadiness and prudence. Though forced to suspend their operations, on some occasions, and seemingly to yield when any formidable confederacy of their vassals united against them, they resumed their measures, as soon as they observed the nobles to be remiss or feeble, and pushed them with vigour. They appointed the royal courts, which originally were ambulatory, and irregular with respect to their times of meeting, to be held in a fixed place, and at stated seasons. They were sollici-tous to name judges of more distinguished abilities than such as presided in the courts of the barons. They added dignity to their character, and splendour to their assemblies. They laboured to render their forms regular, and their decrees consistent. Such judicatories became, of course, the objects of public confidence as well as veneration. The people, relinquishing the partial tribunals of their lords, were eager to bring every subject of contest under the more equal and discerning eye of those whom their sovereign had chosen to give judgment in his name. Thus Kings became once more the heads of the community, and the dispensers of justice to their subjects. The barons, in some kingdoms, ceased to exercise their right of jurisdiction, because it sunk into contempt; in others, it was circumscribed by such regulations as rendered it innocent, or it was entirely abolished by express statutes. Thus the administration of justice taking its rise from one source, and following one direction, held its course in every state with more uniformity, and with greater force.

VI. The forms and maxims of the canon law, which were become universally respectable from their authority in the spiri-tual courts, contributed not a little towards these improvements in jurisprudence which I have enumerated. If the canon law be considered politically, either as a system framed on purpose to assist the clergy in usurping powers and jurisdictions no less repugnant to the nature of their function, than inconsistent with the order of government; or as the chief instrument in establish-ing the dominion of the Popes which shook the throne, and endangered the liberties of every kingdom in Europe, we must pronounce it one of the most formidable engines ever formed against the happiness of civil society. But if we contemplate it merely as a code of laws respecting the rights and property of individuals, and attend only to the civil effects of its decisions con-cerning these, we must view it in a different, and a much more favourable light. In ages of ignorance and credulity, the min-isters of religion are the objects of superstitious veneration. When the barbarians who over-ran the Empire first embraced the Christian faith, they found the clergy in possession of considerable power; and they naturally transferred to these new guides the profound submission and reverence which they were accustomed to yield to the priests of that religion which they had forsaken. They deemed their persons to be as sacred as their function; and would have considered it as impious to subject them to the profane jurisdiction of the laity. The clergy were not blind to the advantages which the weakness of mankind afforded them. They established courts, in which every question relating to their own character, their function, or their property, was tried. They pleaded, and obtained an almost total exemption from the authority of civil judges. Upon different pretexts, and by a multiplicity of artifices, they communicated this privilege to so many persons, and extended their jurisdiction to such a variety of cases, that the greater part of those affairs which give rise to contest and litigation, was drawn under the cognizance of the spiritual courts.

But in order to dispose the laity to suffer these usurpations without murmuring or opposition, it was necessary to convince them, that the administration of justice would be rendered more perfect by the establishment of this new jurisdiction. This was not a difficult undertaking, at the period when the clergy carried on their encroachments with the greatest success. That scanty portion of science which served to guide men in the ages of darkness, was wholly engrossed by the clergy. They alone were accustomed to read, to enquire, and to reason. Whatever knowledge of ancient jurisprudence had been preserved, either by tradition, or in such books as had escaped the destructive rage of barbarians, was possessed only by them. Upon the maxims of that excellent system, they founded a code of laws consonant to the great principles of equity. Being directed by fixed and known rules, the forms of their courts were ascertained, and their decisions became uniform and consistent. Nor did they want authority sufficient to enforce their sentences. Excommunication and other ecclesiastical censures, were punishments more formidable than any that civil judges could inflict in support of their decrees.

It was not surprizing, then, that ecclesiastical jurisprudence should become such an object of admiration and respect; that exemption from civil jurisdiction was courted as a privilege, and conferred as a reward. It is not surprizing, that even to rude people, the maxims of the canon law should appear more equal and just than that ill-digested jurisprudence which directed all proceedings in the civil courts. According to the latter, the differences between contending barons were terminated, as in a state of nature, by the sword; according to the former, every matter was subjected to the decision of laws. The one, by permitting judicial combats, left chance and force to the arbiters of right or wrong, of truth or falsehood; the other, passed judgment with respect to these by the maxims of equity, and the testimony of witnesses. Any error or iniquity in a sentence pronounced by a baron to whom feudal jurisdiction belonged, was irremediable, because originally it was subject to the review of no superior tribunal; the ecclesiastical law established a regular gradation of courts, through all which a cause might be carried by appeal, until it was determined by that authority which was held to be supreme in the church. Thus the genius and principles of the canon law prepared men for approving these three great alterations in the feudal jurisprudence which I have mentioned. But it was not with respect to these points alone that the canon law suggested improvements beneficial to society. Many of the regulations, now deemed the barriers of personal security, or the safeguards of private property, are contrary to the spirit, and repugnant to the maxims of the civil jurisprudence, known in Europe during several centuries, and were borrowed from the rules and practice of the ecclesiastical courts. By observing the wisdom and equity of the decisions in these courts, men began to perceive the necessity either of deserting the martial tribunals of the barons, or of attempting to reform them.

VII. The revival of the knowledge and study of the Roman law, co-operated with the causes which I have mentioned, in introducing more just and liberal ideas concerning the nature of government, and the administration of justice. Among the calamities which the devastations of the barbarians who broke in upon the Empire brought upon mankind, one of the greatest was their overturning the system of Roman jurisprudence, the noblest monument of the wisdom of that great people, formed to subdue and to govern the world. The laws and regulations of a civilized community, were not altogether repugnant to the manners and ideas of these fierce invaders. They had respect to objects, of which a rude people had no conception; and were adapted to a state of society with which they were entirely unacquainted. For this reason, wherever they settled, the Roman jurisprudence soon sunk into oblivion, and lay buried for some centuries under the load of those institutions which the inhabitants of Europe dignified with the name of laws. But towards the middle of the twelfth century, a copy of Justinian's Pandects was accidentally discovered in Italy. By that time, the state of society was so far advanced, and the ideas of men so much enlarged and improved by the occurrences of several centuries, during which they had continued in political union, that they were struck with admiration of a system which their ancestors could not comprehend. Though they had not hitherto attained such a degree of refinement, as to catch from the ancients a relish for true philosophy, or speculative science; though they were still insensible to the beauty and elegance of classical composition; they were sufficiently qualified to judge with respect to the merit of their system of laws, in which all the points most interesting to mankind, and the chief objects of their attention in every age, were settled with discernment, precision and equity. All men of letters studied this new science with eagerness; and within a few years after the discovery of the Pandects, professors of civil law were appointed, who taught it publickly in most countries of Europe.

The effects of having such a perfect model to study and to imitate were soon manifest. Men, as soon as they were acquainted with fixed and general laws, perceived the advantage of them, and became impatient to ascertain the principles and forms by which judges should regulate their decisions. Such was the ardour with which they carried on an undertaking of so great importance to society, that before the close of the twelfth century, the feudal law was reduced into a regular system; the code of canon-law was enlarged and methodized; and the loose uncertain customs of different provinces or kingdoms, were collected and arranged with an order and accuracy acquired from the knowledge of Roman jurisprudence. In some countries of Europe the Roman law was adopted as subsidiary to their own municipal law; and all cases to which the latter did not extend, were decided according to the principles of the former. In others, the maxims as well as forms of Roman jurisprudence mingled imperceptibly with the laws of the country, and had a powerful, though less sensible, influence, in improving and perfecting them.

These various improvements in the system of jurisprudence, and administration of justice, occasioned a change in manners of great importance, and of extensive effect. They gave rise to a distinction of professions; they obliged men to cultivate different talents, and to aim at different accomplishments, in order to qualify themselves for the various departments and functions which became necessary in society.[40] Among uncivilized nations, there is but one profession honourable, that of arms. All the ingenuity and vigour of the human mind are exerted in acquiring military skill, or address. The functions of peace are few and simple; and require no particular course of education or of study, as a preparation for discharging them. This was the state of Europe during several centuries. Every gentleman, born a soldier, scorned any other occupation; he was taught no science but that of war; even his exercises and pastimes were feats of martial prowess. Nor did the judicial character, which persons of noble birth were alone entitled to assume, demand any degree of knowledge beyond that which such untutored soldiers possessed. To recollect a few traditionary customs which time had confirmed, and rendered respectable; to mark out the lists of battle with due formality; to observe the issue of the combat; and to pronounce whether it had been conducted according to the laws of arms; included every thing that a baron who acted as a judge, found it necessary to understand.

But when the forms of legal proceedings were fixed, when the rules of decision were committed to writing, and collected into a body, law became a science, the knowledge of which required a regular course of study, together with long attention to the practice of courts. Martial and illiterate nobles had neither leisure nor inclination to undertake a task so laborious, as well as so foreign from all the occupations which they deemed entertaining, or suitable to their rank. They gradually relinquished their places in courts of justice, where their ignorance exposed them to contempt. They became weary of attending to the discussion of cases, which grew too intricate for them to comprehend. Not only the judicial determination of points which were the subjects of controversy, but the conduct of all legal business and transactions was committed to persons trained by previous study and application to the knowledge of law. An order of men, to whom their fellow-citizens had daily recourse for advice, and to whom they looked up for decision in their most important concerns, naturally acquired consideration and influence in society. They were advanced to honours which had been considered as the peculiar rewards of military virtue. They were entrusted with offices of the highest dignity, and most extensive power. Thus, another profession than that of arms, came to be introduced among the laity, and was reputed honourable. The functions of civil life were attended to. The talents requisite for discharging them were cultivated. A new road was opened to wealth and eminence. The arts and virtues of peace were placed in their proper rank, and received their due recompence.

VIII. While improvements so important with respect to the state of society, and the administration of justice, gradually made progress in Europe, sentiments more liberal and generous had begun to animate the nobles. These were inspired by the spirit of Chivalry, which, though considered, commonly, as a wild institution, the effect of caprice, and the source of extravagance, arose naturally from the state of society at that period, and had a very serious influence in refining the manners of the European nations. The feudal state was a state of perpetual war, rapine, and anarchy; during which the weak and unarmed were exposed every moment to insults or injuries. The power of the sovereign was too limited to prevent these wrongs; and the administration of justice too feeble to redress them. There was scarce any protection against violence and oppression, but what the valour and generosity of private persons afforded. The same spirit of enterprize which had prompted so many gentlemen to take arms in defence of the oppressed pilgrims in Palestine, incited others to declare themselves the patrons and avengers of injured innocence at home. When the final reduction of the Holy Land under the dominion of Infidels put an end to these foreign expeditions, the latter was the only employment left for the activity and courage of adventurers. To check the insolence of overgrown oppressors; to succour the distressed; to rescue the helpless from captivity; to protect, or to avenge women, orphans, and ecclesiastics. who could not bear arms in their own defence; to redress wrongs, and to remove grievances; were deemed acts of the highest prowess and merit. Valour, humanity, courtesy, justice, honour, were the characteristic qualities of chivalry. To these were added religion, which mingled itself with every passion and institution during the middle ages, and by infusing a large proportion of enthusiastic zeal, gave them such force, as carried them to romantic excess. Men were trained to knighthood by a long previous discipline; they were admitted into the order by solemnities no less devout than pompous; every person of noble birth courted that honour; it was deemed a distinction superior to royalty; and monarchs were proud to receive it from the hands of private gentlemen.

This singular institution, in which valour, gallantry, and religion, were so strangely blended, was wonderfully adapted to the taste and genius of martial nobles; and its effects were soon visible in their manners. War was carried on with less ferocity, when humanity came to be deemed the ornament of knighthood no less than courage. More gentle and polished manners were introduced, when courtesy was recommended as the most amiable of knightly virtues. Violence and oppression decreased, when it was reckoned meritorious to check and to punish them. A scrupulous adherence to truth, with the most religious attention to fulfil every engagement, became the distinguishing characteristic of a gentleman, because chivalry was regarded as the school of honour, and inculcated the most delicate sensibility with respect to that point. The admiration of these qualities,

together with the high distinctions and prerogatives conferred
on knighthood in every part of Europe, inspired persons of
noble birth on some occasions with a species of military fanati-
cism, and led them to extravagant enterprizes. But they imprinted
deeply in their minds the principles of generosity and honour.
These were strengthened by every thing that can affect the
senses, or touch the heart. The wild exploits of those romantic
knights who sallied forth in quest of adventures, are well known,
and have been treated with proper ridicule. The political and
permanent effects of the spirit of chivalry have been less observed.
Perhaps, the humanity which accompanies all the operations of
war, the refinements of gallantry, and the point of honour, the
three chief circumstances which distinguish modern from ancient
manners, may be ascribed in a great measure to this whimsical
institution, seemingly of little benefit to mankind. The sentiments which chivalry inspired, had a wonderful influence on
manners and conduct during the twelfth, thirteenth, fourteenth,
and fifteenth centuries. They were so deeply rooted, that they
continued to operate after the vigour and reputation of the
institution itself began to decline. Some considerable transactions,
recorded in the following history, resemble the adventurous
exploits of chivalry, rather than the well regulated operations of
sound policy. Some of the most eminent personages, whose characters will be delineated, were strongly tinctured with this romantic spirit. Francis I was ambitious to distinguish himself by
all the qualities of an accomplished knight, and endeavoured to
imitate the enterprizing genius of chivalry in war, as well as its
pomp and courtesy during peace. The fame which he acquired
by these splendid actions, so far dazzled his more temperate
rival, that he departed on some occasions from his usual prudence and moderation, and emulated Francis in deeds of prowess,
or of gallantry.

IX. The progress of science, and the cultivation of literature,
had considerable effect in changing the manners of the European
nations, and introducing that civility and refinement by which
they are now distinguished. At the time when their Empire was
overturned, the Romans, though they had lost that correct taste

which has rendered the productions of their ancestors the standards of excellence, and models for imitation to succeeding ages, still preserved their love of letters, and cultivated the arts with great ardour. But rude barbarians were so far from being struck with any admiration of these unknown accomplishments, that they despised them. They were not arrived at that state of society, in which those faculties of the human mind, that have beauty and elegance for their objects, begin to unfold themselves. They were strangers to all those wants and desires which are the parents of ingenious invention; and as they did not comprehend either the merit or utility of the Roman arts, they destroyed the monuments of them, with industry not inferior to that with which their posterity have since studied to preserve, or to recover them. The convulsions occasioned by their settlement in the Empire; the frequent as well as violent revolutions in every kingdom which they established; together with the interior defects in the form of government wihch they introduced, banished security and leisure; prevented the growth of taste, or the culture of science; and kept Europe, during several centuries, in that state of ignorance which has been already described. But the events and institutions which I have enumerated, produced great alterations in society. As soon as their operation, in restoring liberty and independance to one part of the community, began to be felt; as soon as they began to communicate to all the members of society some taste of the advantages arising from commerce, from public order, and from personal security, the human mind became conscious of powers which it did not formerly perceive, and fond of occupations or pursuits of which it was formerly incapable. Towards the beginning of the twelfth century, we discern the first symptoms of its awakening from that lethargy in which it had long been sunk, and observe it turning with curiosity and attention towards new objects.

The first literary efforts, however, of the European nations in the middle ages, were extremely ill-directed. Among nations, as well as individuals, the powers of imagination attain some degree of vigour before the intellectual faculties are much exercised in speculative or abstract disquisition. Men are poets before they are philosophers. They feel with sensibility, and describe with force, when they have made but little progress in investigation or reasoning. The age of Homer and of Hesiod long preceded that of Thales, or of Socrates. But, unhappily for literature, our ancestors deviating from this course which nature points out, plunged at once into the depths of abstruse and metaphysical inquiry. They had been converted to the Christian faith, soon after they settled in their new conquests. But they did not receive it pure. The presumption of men had added to the simple and instructive doctrines of Christianity, the theories of a vain philosophy, that attempted to penetrate into mysteries, and to decide questions which the limited faculties of the human mind are unable to comprehend, or to resolve. These over-curious speculations were incorporated with the system of religion, and came to be considered as the most essential part of it. As soon, then, as curiosity prompted men to inquire and to reason, these were the subjects which first presented themselves, and engaged their attention. The scholastic theology, with its infinite train of bold disquisitions, and subtile distinctions concerning points which are not the object of human reason, was the first production of the spirit of enquiry after it began to resume some degree of activity and vigour in Europe. It was not this circumstance alone that gave such a wrong turn to the minds of men, when they began again to exercise talents which they had so long neglected. Most of the persons who attempted to revive literature in the twelfth and thirteenth centuries, had received instruction, or derived their principles of science from the Greeks in the eastern Empire, or from the Arabians in Spain and Africa. Both these people, acute and inquisitive to excess, corrupted those sciences which they cultivated. The former rendered theology a system of speculative refinement, or of endless controversy. The latter communicated to philosophy a spirit of metaphysical and frivolous subtlety. Misled by these guides, the persons who first applied to science were involved in a maze of intricate inquiries. Instead of allowing their fancy to take its natural range, and to produce such works of invention as might have improved their taste, and refined their sentiments; instead of cultivating those arts which embellish human life, and render it comfortable; they were fettered by authority, they were led astray by example, and wasted the whole force of their genius in speculations as unavailing as they were difficult.

But fruitless and ill-directed as these speculations were, their novelty rouzed, and their boldness interested the human mind. The ardour with which men pursued these uninviting studies, was astonishing. Genuine philosophy was never cultivated, in any enlightened age, with greater zeal. Schools, upon the model of these instituted by Charlemagne, were opened in every cathedral, and almost in every monastery of note. Colleges and universities were erected, and formed into communities or corporations, governed by their own laws, and invested with separate and extensive jurisdiction over their own members. A regular course of studies was planned. Privileges of great value were conferred on masters and scholars. Academical titles and honours of various kinds were invented, as a recompence for both. Nor was it in the schools alone that superiority in science led to reputation and authority; it became the object of respect in life, and advanced such as acquired it to a rank of no inconsiderable eminence. Allured by all these advantages, an incredible number of students resorted to these new seats of learning, and crowded with eagerness into that new path which was opened to fame and distinction.

But how considerable soever these first efforts may appear, there was one circumstance which prevented the effects of them from being as extensive as they ought to have been. All the languages in Europe, during the period under review, were barbarous. They were destitute of elegance, of force, and even of perspicuity. No attempt had been hitherto made to improve or to polish them. The Latin tongue was consecrated by the church to religion. Custom, with authority scarce less sacred, had appropriated it to literature. All the sciences cultivated in the twelfth and thirteenth centuries, were taught in Latin. All books with respect to them were written in that language. To have treated of any important subject in a modern language, would have been deemed a degradation of it. This confined science within a very narrow circle. The learned alone were admitted into the temple of knowledge; the gate was shut against all others, who were allowed to remain involved in their former darkness and ignorance.

But though science was thus prevented, during several ages, from diffusing itself through society, and its influence was circumscribed; the progress of it may be mentioned, nevertheless, among the great causes which contributed to introduce a change of manners into Europe. That ardent, though ill-judged spirit of enquiry which I have described, occasioned a fermentation of mind which put ingenuity and invention in motion, and gave them vigour. It led men to a new employment of their faculties, which they found to be agreeable as well as interesting. It accustomed them to exercises and occupations which tended to soften their manners, and to give them some relish for those gentle virtues, which are peculiar to nations among whom science hath been cultivated with success.

X. The progress of commerce had considerable influence in polishing the manners of the European nations, and in leading them to order, equal laws, and humanity. The wants of men, in the original and most simple state of society, are so few, and their desires so limited, that they rest contented with the natural productions of their climate and soil, or with what they can add to these by their own rude industry. They have no superfluities to dispose of, and few necessities that demand a supply. Every little community subsisting on its own domestick stock, and satisfied with it, is either unacquainted with the states around it, or at variance with them. Society and manners must be considerably improved, and many provisions must be made for public order and personal security, before a liberal intercourse can take place between different nations. We find, accordingly, that the first effect of the settlement of the barbarians in the Empire, was to divide those nations which the Roman power had united. Europe was broken into many separate communities. The communication between these divided states ceased almost totally during several centuries. Navigation was dangerous in seas infested by pirates; nor could strangers trust to a friendly reception in the ports of uncivilized nations. Even between distant parts of the same kingdom, the intercourse was rare and difficult. The lawless rapine of banditti, together with the avowed exactions of the nobles, scarce less formidable and oppressive, rendered a journey of any length a perilous enterprize. Fixed to the spot in which they resided, the greater part of the inhabitants of Europe lost, in a great measure, the knowledge of remote regions, and were unacquainted with their names, their situations, their climates, and their commodities.

Various causes, contributed to revive the spirit of commerce, and to renew in some degree the intercourse between different nations. The Italians, by their connection with Constantinople and other cities of the Greek empire, preserved in their own country some relish for the precious commodities, and curious manufactures of the East. They communicated some knowledge of these to the countries contiguous to Italy. This commerce, however, was extremely limited, nor was the intercourse considerable which it occasioned between different nations. The Crusades, by leading multitudes from every corner of Europe into Asia, opened a more extensive communication between the East and West, which subsisted for two centuries; and though the object of these expeditions was conquest and not commerce; though the issue of them proved as unfortunate, as the motives for undertaking them were wild and enthusiastic, their commercial effects, as hath been shewn, were both beneficial and permanent. During the continuance of the Crusades, the great cities in Italy and in other countries of Europe acquired liberty, and together with it such privileges as rendered them respectable and independant communities. Thus, in every state there was formed a new order of citizens, to whom commerce presented itself as their proper object, and opened to them a certain path to wealth and dignity. Soon after the close of the Holy war, the mariner's compass was invented, which, by rendering navigation more secure as well as more adventrous, facilitated the communication between remote nations, and brought them nearer to each other.

The Italian States, during the same period, established a

regular commerce with the East in the ports of Egypt, and drew from thence all the rich products of the Indies. They introduced into their own territories manufactures of various kinds, and carried them on with great ingenuity and vigour. They attempted new arts; and transplanted from warmer climates, to which they had been hitherto deemed peculiar, several natural productions which now furnish the materials of a lucrative and extended commerce. All these commodities, whether imported from Asia, or produced by their own skill, they disposed of to great advantage among the other people of Europe, who, began to acquire some taste of elegance unknown to their ancestors, or despised by them. During the twelfth and thirteenth centuries, the commerce of Europe was almost entirely in the hands of the Italians, more commonly known in those ages by the name of Lombards. Companies or societies of Lombard merchants settled in every different kingdom. They were taken under the immediate protection of the several governments. They enjoyed extensive privileges and immunities. The operation of the ancient barbarous laws concerning strangers was suspended with respect to them. They became the carriers, the manufacturers, and the bankers of all Europe.

While the Italians, in the south of Europe, cultivated trade with such industry and success, the commercial spirit awakened in the north, towards the middle of the thirteenth century. As the nations around the Baltick were, at that time, extremely barbarous, and infested that sea with their piracies, this obliged the cities of Lubeck and Hamburgh, soon after they began to open some trade with these people, to enter into a league of mutual defence. They derived such advantages from this union, that other towns acceded to their confederacy, and, in a short time, eighty of the most considerable cities scattered through those vast countries which stretch from the bottom of the Baltick to Cologne on the Rhine, joined in the famous Hanseatick league, which became so formidable, that its alliance was courted, and its enmity was dreaded by the greatest monarchs. The members of this powerful association formed the first systematick plan of commerce known in the middle ages, and conducted it by common laws enacted in their general assemblies. They supplied the rest of Europe with naval stores, and pitched on different towns, the most eminent of which was Bruges in Flanders, where they established staples in which their commerce was regularly carried on. Thither the Lombards brought the productions of India, together with the manufactures of Italy, and exchanged them for the more bulky, but not less useful commodities of the North. The Hanseatick merchants disposed of the cargoes which they received from the Lombards, in the ports of the Baltick, or carried them up the great rivers into the interior parts of Germany.

This regular intercourse opened between the North and South of Europe made them sensible of their mutual wants, and created such new and vast demands for commodities of every kind, that it excited among the inhabitants of the Netherlands a more vigorous spirit in carrying on the two great manufactures of wool and flax, which seem to have been considerable in that country as far back as the age of Charlemagne. As Bruges became the centre of communication between the Lombard and Hanseatick merchants, the Flemings traded with both in that city to such extent as well as advantage as spread among them a general habit of industry, which long rendered Flanders and the adjacent provinces the most opulent, the most populous, and best cultivated countries in Europe.

Struck with the flourishing state of these provinces, of which he discerned the true cause, Edward III of England, endeavoured to excite a spirit of industry among his own subjects, who, blind to the advantages of their situation, and ignorant of the source from which opulence was destined to flow into their country, totally neglected commerce, and did not even attempt those manufactures, the materials of which they furnished to foreigners. By alluring Flemish artisans to settle in his dominions, as well as by many wise laws for the encouragement and regulation of trade, he gave a beginning to the woolen manufactures of England, and first turned the active and enterprizing genius of his people towards those arts which have raised the English to the highest rank among commercial nations.

66

This increase of commerce, and of intercourse between nations, how inconsiderable soever it may appear in respect of their rapid and extensive progress during the last and present age, seems vast, when we compare it with the state of both in Europe previous to the twelfth century. It did not fail of producing great effects. Commerce tends to wear off those prejudices which maintain distinction and animosity between nations. It softens and polishes the manners of men. It unites them, by one of the strongest of all ties, the desire of supplying their mutual wants. It disposes them to peace, by establishing in every state an order of citizens bound by their interest to be the guardians of publick tranquillity. As soon as the commercial spirit begins to acquire vigour, and to gain an ascendant in any society, we discover a new genius in its policy, its alliances, its wars, and its negociations. Conspicuous proofs of this occur in the history of the Italian States, of the Hanseatick league, and the cities of the Netherlands during the period under review. In proportion as commerce made its way into the different countries of Europe, they successively turned their attention to those objects, and adopted those manners, which occupy and distinguish polished nations.*

---

* See note beginning on p. 165, Proofs and Illustrations.—Editor.

II

The Command of the National Force Requisite in Foreign Operations

Such are the events and institutions, which by their powerful operation contributed, gradually, to introduce more regular government and more polished manners into the various nations of Europe. When we survey the state of society, or the character of individuals, at the opening of the fifteenth century, and then turn back to view the condition of both at the time when the barbarous tribes which overturned the Roman power completed their settlement in their new conquests, the progress which mankind had made towards order and refinement will appear immense.

Government, however, was still far from having attained that state, in which extensive monarchies act with united vigour, or carry on great undertakings with perseverance and success. Small tribes or communities, even in their rudest state, may operate in concert, and exert their utmost force. They are excited to act not by the distant objects, and subtile speculations, which interest or affect men in polished societies, but by their present feelings. The insults of an enemy kindle resentment; the success of a rival tribe awakens emulation; these passions communicate from breast to breast, and all the members of the community, with united ardour, rush into the field in order to gratify their revenge, or to acquire distinction. But in widely extended states, such as the great kingdoms of Europe at the beginning of the fifteenth century, where there is little intercourse between the distant members of the community, and where every great enter-prize requires previous concert and long preparation, nothing can rouse and call forth their united strength, but the absolute com-mand of a Despot, or the powerful influence of regular policy. Of the former the vast Empires in the East are an example; the irresistible mandate of the Sovereign reaches the most remote provinces of his dominions, and compels whatever number of his subjects he is pleased to summon, to follow his standard. The kingdoms of Europe, in the present age, are an instance of the latter; the Prince, by the less violent, but no less effectual opera-tion of laws and a well regulated government, is enabled to avail himself of the whole force of his state, and to employ it in enterprizes which require strenuous and persevering efforts.

But, at the opening of the fifteenth century, the political constitution in all the kingdoms of Europe was very different from either of these states of government. The several monarchs, though they had somewhat enlarged the boundaries of preroga-tive by successful encroachments on the immunities and privi-leges of the nobility, were possessed of an authority extremely limited. The laws and interior police of kingdoms, though much improved by the various events and regulations which I have enumerated, were still feeble and imperfect. In every country, a numerous body of nobles, still formidable notwithstanding the various expedients employed to depress them, watched all the motions of their sovereign with a jealous attention, which set bounds to his ambition, and either prevented his forming schemes of extensive enterprize, or thwarted the execution of them.

The ordinary revenues of every Prince were so extremely small as to be inadequate to any great undertaking. He depended for extraordinary supplies on the good will of his subjects, who granted them often with a reluctant and always with a sparing hand.

As the revenues of Princes were inconsiderable, the armies which they could bring into the field were unfit for long and effectual service. Instead of being able to employ troops trained to skill in arms, and to military subordination, by regular discipline, Monarchs were obliged to depend on such forces as their vassals conducted to their standard in consequence of their military tenures. These, as they were bound to remain under arms only for a short time, could not march far from their usual place of residence, and being more attached to the lord of whom they held, than to the Sovereign whom they served, were often as much disposed to counteract as to forward his schemes. Nor were they, even if they had been more subject to the command of the monarch, proper instruments to carry into execution any great and arduous enterprize. The strength of an army formed either for conquest or defence lies in infantry. To the stability and discipline of their legions, consisting chiefly of infantry, the Romans during the times of the republick were indebted for all their victories; and when their descendants, forgetting the institutions which had led them to universal dominion, so far altered their military system as to place their principal confidence in a numerous cavalry, the undisciplined impetuosity of the barbarous nations who fought mostly on foot, was sufficient, as I have already observed, to overcome them. These nations soon after they settled in their new conquests, uninstructed by the fatal error of the Romans, relinquished the customs of their ancestors and converted the chief force of their armies into cavalry. Among the Romans this change was occasioned by the effeminacy of their troops, who could not endure the fatigues of service, which their more virtuous and hardy ancestors sustained with ease. Among the people who established the new monarchies into which Europe was divided, this innovation in military discipline seems to have flowed from the pride of the nobles, who scorning to mingle with persons of inferior rank, aimed at being distinguished from them in the field as well as during peace. The institution of chivalry, and the frequency of Tournaments, in which knights, in complete armour, entered the lists on horseback with extraordinary splendour, displaying amazing address, and force, and valour, brought cavalry into still greater esteem. The fondness for that service increased to such a degree, that, during the thirteenth and fourteenth centuries, the armies of Europe were composed almost entirely of cavalry. No gentleman would appear in the field but on horseback. To serve in any other manner he would have deemed derogatory to his rank. The cavalry, by way of distinction, was called, *The battle,* and on it alone depended the fate of every action. The infantry, collected from the dregs and refuse of the people, ill armed and worse disciplined, was of no account.

As these circumstances rendered the operations of particular kingdoms less considerable and less vigorous, so they long kept the Princes of Europe from giving such attention to the schemes and transactions of their neighbours, as led them to form any regular system of publick security. They prevented them from uniting in confederacy, or from acting with concert, in order to establish such a distribution and balance of power, as should hinder any state from rising to a superiority, which might endanger the general liberty and independance. During several centuries, the nations of Europe appear to have considered themselves as separate societies, scarce connected together by any common interest, and little concerned in each others affairs or operations. An extensive commerce did not afford them an opportunity of observing and penetrating into the schemes of every different state. They had not ambassadors residing constantly in every court to watch and give early intelligence of all its motions. The expectation of remote advantages, or the prospect of distant and contingent evils were not sufficient to excite nations to take arms. They only, who were within the sphere of immediate danger, and unavoidably exposed to injury or insult, thought themselves interested in any contest, or bound to take precautions for their own safety.

Whoever records the transactions of any of the more considerable European states during the two last centuries, must write the history of Europe. Its various kingdoms, throughout that period, have been formed into one great system, so closely united, that each holding a determinate station, the operations of one are so felt by all, as to influence their counsels and regulate their measures. But previous to the fifteenth century, unless when vicinity of territory rendered the occasions of discord frequent and unavoidable, or when national emulation fomented or embittered the spirit of hostility, the affairs of different countries are seldom interwoven. In each kingdom of Europe great events and revolutions happened, which the other powers beheld with the same indifference as if they had been uninterested spectators, to whom the effect of these transactions could never extend.

During the violent struggles between France and England, and notwithstanding the alarming progress which was made towards rendering one Prince the master of both these kingdoms, hardly one measure which can be considered as the result of a sagacious and prudent policy, was formed in order to guard against an event so fatal to Europe. The Dukes of Burgundy and Bretagne, whom their situation would not permit to remain neutral, engaged, it is true, in the contest; but they more frequently took the part to which their passions prompted them, than that which a just discernment of the danger which threatened themselves and the tranquillity of Europe should have pointed out. The other Princes, seemingly unaffected by the alternate successes of the contending parties, left them to decide the quarrel, or interposed only by feeble and ineffectual negociations.

Notwithstanding the perpetual hostilities in which the various kingdoms of Spain were engaged during several centuries, and the successive occurrences which visibly tended to unite that part of the continent into one great monarchy, the Princes of Europe scarce took a single step, which discovers that they gave any attention to that important event. They permitted a power to arise imperceptibly, and to acquire strength there, which soon became formidable to all its neighbours.

Amidst the violent convulsions with which the spirit of domination in the See of Rome, and the turbulent ambition of the German nobles, agitated the Empire, neither the authority of the Popes, seconded by all their artifices and intrigues, nor the sollicitations of the Emperors, could induce any of the powerful monarchs in Europe to engage in their quarrel, or to avail themselves of many favourable opportunities of interposing with effect and advantage.

This amazing inactivity, during transactions so interesting, is not to be imputed to any incapacity of discerning their political consequences. The power of judging with sagacity, and of acting with vigour, is the portion of the men in every age. The Monarchs who reigned in the different kingdoms of Europe during several centuries were not blind to their particular interest, negligent of the publick safety, or strangers to the method of securing both. If they did not adopt that salutary system, which teaches modern politicians to take the alarm at the prospect of distant dangers, which prompts them to check the first encroachments of any formidable power, and which renders each state the guardian, in some degree, of the rights and independance of all its neighbours, this was owing entirely to the imperfections and disorders in the civil government of each country, which made it impossible for sovereigns to act suitably to those ideas which the posture of affairs, and their own observation must have suggested.

But during the course of the fifteenth century, various events happened, which, by giving Princes more entire command of the force in their respective dominions, rendered their operations more vigorous and extensive. In consequence of this, the affairs of different kingdoms becoming more frequently as well as more intimately connected, they were gradually accustomed to act in concert and confederacy, and were insensibly prepared for forming a system of policy, in order to establish or to preserve such a balance of power as was most consistent with the general security. It was during the reign of Charles the fifth, that the ideas, on which this system is founded, first came to be fully understood. It was then, that the maxims by which it has been uniformly maintained since that æra were universally adopted. On this account, a view of the causes and events which contributed to establish a plan of policy more salutary and extensive than any that has taken place in the conduct of human affairs, is not only a necessary introduction to the following work, but is a capital object in the history of Europe.

The first event, that occasioned any considerable alteration in the arrangement of affairs in Europe, was the annexation of the extensive territories, which England possessed on the continent, to the crown of France. While the English were masters of several of the most fertile and opulent provinces in France, and a great part of its most martial inhabitants were bound to follow their standard, their monarchs considered themselves rather as the rivals, than as the vassals of the sovereign of whom they held. The Kings of France, circumscribed and thwarted in their schemes and operations by an adversary no less jealous than formidable, durst not venture upon any enterprize of importance or of difficulty. The English were always at hand, ready to oppose them. They disputed even their right to their crown, and being able to penetrate, with ease, into the heart of the kingdom, could arm against them those very hands which ought to have been employed in their defence. Timid counsels, and feeble efforts were natural to monarchs in such a situation. France, dismembred and over-awed, could not attain its proper station in the system of Europe. But the death of Henry of England, happily for France, and not unfortunately for his own country, delivered the French from the calamity of having a foreign master seated on their throne. The weakness of a long minority, the dissensions in the English court, together with the unsteady and languid conduct which these occassioned, afforded the French a favourable opportunity of recovering the territories which they had lost. The native valour of the nobility of France, heightened to an enthusiastic confidence, by a supposed interposition of heaven in their behalf; conducted in the field by skilful leaders; and directed in the cabinet by a prudent monarch; was exerted with such vigour and success, during this favourable juncture, as not only wrested from the English their new conquests, but stript them of their ancient possessions, and reduced them within the narrow precincts of Calais, and its petty territory.

As soon as so many considerable provinces were re-united to their dominions, the Kings of France, conscious of this acquisition of strength, began to form bolder schemes of interior policy, as well as of foreign operations. They immediately became formidable to their neighbours, who began to fix their attention on their measures and motions, the importance of which they fully perceived. From this æra, France, possessed of the advantages which it derives from the situation and contiguity of its territories, as well as from the number and valour of its people, rose to new influence in Europe, and was the first power in a condition to give alarm to the jealousy or fears of the states around it.

Nor was France indebted for this increase of importance merely to the re-union of the provinces which had been torn from it. A circumstance attended the recovery of these, which, though less considerable, and less observed, contributed not a little to give additional vigour and decision to all the efforts of that monarchy. During the obstinate struggles between France and England, all the defects of the military system under the feudal government were sensibly felt. A war of long continuance languished, when carried on by troops bound and accustomed to keep the field only for a few weeks. Armies, composed chiefly of heavy armed cavalry, were unfit either for the attack or the defence of the many towns and castles, which it became necessary to guard or to reduce. In order to obtain such permanent and effective force, as became requisite during these lengthened contests, the Kings of France took into their pay considerable bands of mercenary soldiers, levied sometimes among their own subjects, and sometimes in foreign countries. But as the feudal policy provided no sufficient funds for such extraordinary service, these adventurers were dismissed at the close of every campaign, or upon any prospect of accommodation; and having been little accustomed to the restraints of discipline, they frequently turned their arms against the country which they had been hired to defend, and desolated it with no less cruelty than its foreign enemies.

A body of troops kept constantly on foot, and regularly trained to military subordination, would have supplied what was wanting in the feudal constitution, and have furnished Princes with the means of executing enterprizes, to which they were then unequal. Such an establishment, however, was so repugnant to the genius of feudal policy, and so incompatible with the privileges and pretensions of the nobles, that during several centuries no monarch was either so bold, or so powerful, as to venture on any step towards introducing it. At last, Charles VII availing himself of the reputation which he had acquired by his successes against the English, and taking advantage of the impressions of terror which such a formidable enemy had left upon the minds of his subjects, executed that which his predecessors durst not attempt. Under pretence of keeping always on foot a force sufficient to defend the kingdom against any sudden invasion of the English, he, at the time when he disbanded his other troops, retained under arms a body of nine thousand cavalry, and of sixteen thousand infantry. He appropriated funds for the regular payment of these; he stationed them in different places of the kingdom, according to his pleasure; and appointed the officers, who commanded and disciplined them. The prime nobility courted this service, in which they were taught to depend on their sovereign, to execute his orders, and to look up to him as the judge and rewarder of their merit. The feudal militia, composed of the vassals whom the nobles could call out to follow their standard, as it was in no degree comparable to a body of soldiers regularly trained to war, sunk gradually in reputation. The strength of armies came to be estimated only by the number of disciplined men which they contained. In less than a century, the nobles and their military tenants, though sometimes summoned to the field, according to ancient form, were considered as an incumbrance upon the troops with which they acted; and were viewed with contempt by soldiers accustomed to the vigorous and steady operations of regular service.

Thus the regulations of Charles the seventh, by establishing the first standing army known in Europe, occasioned an important revolution in its affairs and policy. By depriving the nobles of that direction of the military force of the state, which had raised them to such high authority and importance, it gave a deep wound to the feudal aristocracy, in that part where its power seemed to be most complete.

France, by forming this body of regular troops, at a time when there was scarce a squadron or company kept in constant pay in any other part of Europe, acquired such advantages, either for attack or defence, over its neighbours, that self-preservation made it necessary for them to imitate its examples. Mercenary troops were introduced into all the considerable kingdoms on the continent. They gradually became the only military force that was employed or trusted. It has long been the chief object of policy to increase and to support them, and the great aim of Princes or ministers to discredit and to annihilate all other means of national activity or defence.

As the Kings of France got the start of other powers in establishing in their dominions a military force, which enabled them to carry on foreign operations with more vigour, and to greater extent, so they were the first who effectually broke the feudal aristocracy, and humbled the great vassals of the crown, who by their exorbitant power had long circumscribed the royal prerogative within very narrow limits, and had rendered all the efforts of the monarchs of Europe inconsiderable. Many things concurred to undermine, gradually, the power of the feudal aristocracy in France. The wealth and property of the nobility were greatly impaired during the long wars, which the kingdom was obliged to maintain with the English. The extraordinary zeal with which they exerted themselves in defence of their country against its ancient enemies, exhausted the fortunes of some great families. As almost every province in the kingdom was, in its turn, the seat of war, the lands of others were exposed to the depredations of the enemy, were ravaged by the mercenary troops which their sovereigns hired occasionally, but could not pay, or were desolated with rage still more destructive by the peasants, in their different insurrections. At the same time, the necessities of government having forced their Kings upon the desperate expedient of making great and sudden alterations in the current coin of the kingdom, the fines, quit-rents, and other payments, fixed by ancient custom, sunk much in value, and the revenues of a fief were reduced far below the sum which it had once yielded. During their contests with the English, in which a generous nobility courted every station where danger appeared, or honour could be gained, many families of note became extinct, and their fiefs were reunited to the crown. Other fiefs, in a long course of years, fell to female heirs, and were divided among them; were diminished by profuse donations to the church, or were broken and split by the succession of remote collateral heirs.[1]

Encouraged by these manifest symptoms of decline in that body which he wished to depress, Charles VII during the first interval of peace with England, made several efforts towards establishing the regal prerogative on the ruins of the aristocracy. But his obligations to the nobles were so many, as well as recent, and their services in recovering the kingdom so splendid, as made it necessary for him to proceed with moderation and caution. Such, however, was the authority which the crown had acquired by the progress of its arms against the English, and so much was the power of the nobility diminished, that, without any opposition, he soon made innovations of great consequence in the constitution. He not only established that formidable body of regular troops, which has been mentioned, but he was the first monarch of France who, by his royal edict, without the concurrence of the States-general of the kingdom, levied an extraordinary subsidy on his people. He prevailed likewise with his subjects to render several taxes perpetual, which had formerly been imposed occasionally, and exacted during a short time. By means of all these, he acquired such an increase of power, and extended his prerogative so far beyond its ancient limits, that, from being the most dependant Prince who had ever sat upon the throne of France, he came to possess, during the latter years of his reign, a degree of authority which none of his predecessors had enjoyed for several ages.[2]

That plan of humbling the nobility which Charles formed, his son Louis XI carried on with a bolder spirit, and with greater success. Louis was formed by nature to be a tyrant; and at whatever period he had been called to ascend the throne, his reign must have abounded with schemes to oppress his people, and to render his own power absolute. Subtle, unfeeling, cruel; a stranger to every principle of integrity, and regardless of decency, he scorned all the restraints which a sense of honour, or the desire of fame, impose even on ambitious men. Sagacious, at the same time, to discern his true interest, and influenced by that alone, he was capable of pursuing it with a persevering industry, and of adhering to it with a systematic spirit from which no object could divert, and no danger could deter him.

The maxims of his administration were as profound as they were fatal to the privileges of the nobility. He filled all the departments of government with new men and often with persons, whom he called from the lowest as well as most despised functions in life, and raised at pleasure to stations of great power or trust. These were his only confidents, whom he consulted in forming his plans, and to whom he committed the execution of them: While the nobles, accustomed to be the companions, the favourites, and the ministers of their sovereigns, were treated with such studied and mortifying neglect, that if they would not submit to follow a court, in which they appeared without any shadow of their ancient power, they were obliged to retire to their castles, where they remained unemployed and forgotten. Not satisfied with having rendered the nobles of less consideration, by taking out of their hands the sole direction of affairs, Louis added insult to neglect; and by violating their most valuable privileges, endeavoured to degrade the order, and to reduce the members of it to the same level with other subjects. Persons of the highest rank among them, if so bold as to oppose his schemes, or so unfortunate as to awaken the jealousy of his capricious temper, were prosecuted with rigour, from which all who belonged to the order of nobles had hitherto been exempt; they were tried by judges who had no right to take cognizance of their actions; and were subjected to torture, or condemned to an infamous death, without regard to their birth or condition. The people, accustomed to see the blood of the most illustrious personages shed by the hands of the common executioner, to behold them shut up in dungeons, and carried about in cages of iron, began to view the nobility with less reverence than formerly, and looked up with terror to the royal authority, which seemed to have humbled or annihilated every other power in the kingdom.

At the same time, Louis, being afraid that opposition might rouze the nobles, whom the rigour of his government had intimidated, or that self-preservation might teach them, at last, to unite, dexterously scattered among them the seeds of discord; and industriously fomented those ancient animosities between the great families, which the spirit of jealousy and emulation, natural to the feudal government, had originally kindled and still kept alive. To accomplish this, all the arts of intrigue, all the mysteries and refinements of his fraudulent policy were employed, and with such success, that at a juncture which required the most strenuous efforts, as well as the most perfect union, the nobles never acted, except during one short sally of resentment at the beginning of his reign, either with vigour or with concert.

As he stripped the nobility of their privileges, he added to the power and prerogative of the crown. In order to have at command such a body of soldiers as might be sufficient to crush any force that his disaffected subjects could draw together, he not only kept on foot the regular troops which his father had raised, but took into his pay six thousand Swiss, the best disciplined and most formidable infantry, at that time, in Europe.[3] From the jealousy natural to tyrants, he confided in these foreign mercenaries, as the most devoted instruments of oppression, and the most faithful guardians of the power which he had acquired.

Great funds were requisite, not only to defray the expence of this additional establishment, but to supply the sums employed in the various enterprizes which the restless activity of his genius prompted him to undertake. But the prerogative that his father had assumed of levying taxes, without the concurrence of the states-general, which he was careful not only to retain but to extend, enabled him to provide in some measure for the increasing charges of government.

What his prerogative, enlarged as it was, could not furnish, his address procured. He was the first monarch in Europe who discovered the method of managing those great assemblies, in which the feudal policy had vested the power of granting subsidies and of imposing taxes. He first taught other Princes the fatal art of beginning their attack on publick liberty, by corrupting the source from which it should flow. By exerting all his power and address in influencing the election of representatives, by bribing or overawing the members, and by various changes which he artfully made in the form of their deliberations, Louis acquired such entire direction of these assemblies, that, from being the vigilant guardians of the privileges and property of the people, he rendered them tamely subservient, in promoting the most odious measures of his reign.[4] As no power remained to set bounds to his exactions, he not only continued all the taxes imposed by his father, but made immense additions to them, which amounted to a sum that appeared astonishing to his contemporaries.[5]

Nor was it the power alone or wealth of the crown that Louis increased; he extended its territories by acquisitions of various kinds. He got possession of Rousillon by purchase; Provence was conveyed to him by the will of Charles de Anjou; and upon the death of Charles the Bold, he seized with a strong hand Burgundy and Artois, which had belonged to that Prince. Thus, during the course of a single reign, France was formed into one compact kingdom, and the steady unrelenting policy of Louis XI not only subdued the haughty spirit of the feudal nobles, but established a species of government, scarce less absolute, or less terrible, than eastern despotism.

But fatal as his administration was to the liberties of his subjects, the authority which he acquired, the resources of which he became master, and his freedom from restraint both in concerting his plans and in executing them, rendered his reign active and enterprizing. Louis negociated in all the courts of Europe; he observed the motions of all his neighbours; he engaged, either as principal, or as an auxiliary, in every great transaction; his resolutions were prompt; his operations vigorous; and upon every emergence he could call forth into action the whole force of his kingdom. From the æra of his reign, instead of the feeble efforts of monarchs fettered and circumscribed by a jealous nobility, the Kings of France, more masters at home, have exerted themselves more abroad, have formed more extensive schemes of foreign conquests, and have carried on war with a spirit and vigour long unknown in Europe.

The example which Louis set was too inviting not to be imitated by other Princes. Henry VII as soon as he was seated on the throne of England, formed the plan of enlarging his own prerogative, by breaking the power of the nobility. The circumstances under which he undertook to execute it, were less favourable than those under which Charles VII had made the same attempt; and the spirit with which he conducted it, was very different from that of Louis XI. Charles, by the success of his arms against the English, by the merit of having expelled them out of so many provinces, had established himself so firmly in the confidence of his people, as encouraged him to make bold encroachments on the ancient constitution. The daring genius of Louis broke through every barrier, and endeavoured to overturn or to remove every obstacle that stood in his way. But Henry held the sceptre by a disputed title; a popular faction was ready every moment to take arms against him; and after long civil wars, during which the nobility had often displayed their power in creating and deposing Kings, he felt that the regal authority had been so much relaxed, and that he entered into possession of a prerogative so much abridged, as made it necessary to carry on his measures deliberately, and without any violent exertion. He endeavoured to undermine that formidable structure, which he durst not attack with open force. His schemes, though cautious and slow in their operation, were prudent, and productive in the end of great effects. By his laws, permitting the barons to break the entails of their estates, and to expose them to sale; by his regulations to prevent the nobility from keeping in their service those numerous bands of retainers, which rendered them formidable, and turbulent; by encouraging population, agriculture and commerce; by securing to his subjects, during a long reign, the enjoyment of the blessings which flow from the arts of peace, by accustoming them to an administration of government, under which the laws were executed with steadiness and vigour; he made imperceptibly such alterations in the English constitution, that he transmitted to his successor authority so extensive, as rendered him one of the most absolute Monarchs in Europe, and capable of the greatest and most vigorous efforts.

In Spain, the union of all its crowns by the marriage of Ferdinand and Isabella; the glory that they acquired by the conquest of Granada, which brought the odious dominion of the Moors to a period; the command of the great armies which it had been necessary to keep constantly on foot, in order to accomplish this;

the wisdom and steadiness of their administration; and the address with which they availed themselves of every incident to humble the nobility, and to extend their own prerogative, conspired in raising these monarchs to such eminence and and authority, as none of their predecessors had ever enjoyed. Though several causes, which shall be explained in another place, prevented their attaining the same extensive powers with the Kings of France and England, and preserved the feudal constitution in Spain longer entire, their great abilities supplied the defects of their prerogative, and improved with such dexterity all the advantages which they possessed, that Ferdinand carried on all his foreign operations, which were very extensive, with extraordinary vigour and effect.

While these Princes were thus enlarging the boundaries of prerogative, and taking such steps towards rendering their kingdoms capable of acting with union and with force, events occurred, which called them forth to exert the new powers which they had acquired. These engaged them in such a series of enterprizes and negociations, that the affairs of all the considerable nations in Europe came to be insensibly interwoven with each other; and a great political system was gradually formed, which grew to be an object of universal attention.

The first event which merits notice, on account of its influence in producing this change in the state of Europe, was the marriage of the daughter of Charles the Bold, the sole heiress of the house of Burgundy. For some years before her father's death, she had been considered as the apparent successor to his territories, and Charles had made proposals of marrying her to several different Princes, with a view of alluring them, by that offer, to favour the schemes which his restless ambition was continually forming.

This rendered the alliance with her an object of general attention; and all the advantages of acquiring possession of her territories, the most opulent at that time and best cultivated of any on this side of the Alps, were perfectly understood. As soon, then, as the untimely death of Charles opened the succession, the eyes of all the Princes in Europe were turned towards Mary, and they felt themselves deeply interested in the choice which she was about to make of the person, on whome she would bestow that rich inheritance.

Louis XI from whose kingdom several of the provinces which she possessed had been dismembred, and whose dominions stretched along the frontier of her territories, had every inducement to court her alliance. He had, likewise, a good title to expect the favourable reception of any reasonable proposition he should make, with respect to the disposal of a Princess, who was the vassal of his crown, and descended from the royal blood of France. There were only two propositions, however, which he could make with propriety. The one was the marriage of the Dauphin, the other that of the Count of Angouleme, a Prince of the blood, with the heiress of Burgundy. By the former, he would have annexed all her territories to his crown, and have rendered France at once the most respectable monarchy in Europe. But the great disparity of age between the two parties, Mary being twenty, and the Dauphin only eight years old; the avowed resolution of the Flemings, not to chuse a master possessed of such power as might enable him to form schemes dangerous to their liberties; together with their dread of falling under the odious and oppressive government of Louis, were obstacles in the way of executing this plan, which it was vain to think of surmounting. By the latter, the accomplishment of which might have been attained with ease, Mary having discovered some inclination to a match with the Count of Angouleme,[6] Louis would have prevented the dominions of the house of Burgundy from being conveyed to a rival power, and in return for such a splendid establishment for the Count of Angouleme, he must have obtained, or would have extorted from him concessions highly beneficial to the crown of France. But Louis had been accustomed so long to the intricacies of a crooked and insidious policy, that he could not be satisfied with what was obvious and simple; and was so fond of artifice and refinement, that he came to consider these as his ultimate object, not as the means only of conducting affairs. From this principle, no less than from his unwillingness to aggrandize any of his own subjects, or from his desire of oppressing the house of Burgundy, which he hated, he neglected the

84

course which a Prince less able and artful would have taken, and followed one more suited to his own genius.

He proposed to render himself master, by force of arms, of those provinces, which Mary held of the crown of France, and even to push his conquests into her other territories, while he amused her with insisting continually on the impracticable match with the Dauphin. In prosecuting this plan, he displayed wonderful talents and industry, and exhibited such scenes of treachery, falsehood and cruelty, as are amazing even in the history of Louis XI. Immediately upon the death of Charles, he put his troops in motion, and advanced towards the Netherlands. He corrupted the leading men in the provinces of Burgundy and Artois, and seduced them to desert their sovereign. He got admission into some of the frontier towns by bribing the governors; the gates of others were opened to him in consequence of his intrigues with the inhabitants. He negotiated with Mary; and, in order to render her odious to her subjects, he betrayed to them her most important secrets. He carried on a private correspondence with the two ministers whom she chiefly trusted, and then communicated the letters which he had received from them to the states of Flanders, who, enraged at their perfidy, brought them immediately to trial, tortured them with most extreme cruelty, and, unmoved by the tears and intreaties of their sovereign, who knew and approved of all that the ministers had done, they beheaded them in her presence.[7]

While Louis, by his conduct, unworthy of a great monarch, was securing the possession of Burgundy, Artois, and the towns on the Somme, the states of Flanders carried on a negociation with the Emperor Frederick III and concluded a treaty of marriage between their sovereign and his son Maximilian, Archduke of Austria. The illustrious birth of that Prince, as well as the high dignity of which he had the prospect, rendered the alliance honourable for Mary, while, from the distance of his hereditary territories, and the scantiness of his revenues, his power was so inconsiderable as did not excite the jealousy or fear of the Flemings.

Thus Louis, by the caprice of his temper, and the excess of

his refinements, put the house of Austria in possession of this noble inheritance. By this acquisition, the foundation of the future grandeur of Charles V was laid; and he became master of those territories, which enabled him to carry on his most formidable and decisive operations against France. Thus, too, the same monarch who first united the interior force of France, and established it on such a footing as to render it formidable to the rest of Europe, contributed, far contrary to his intention, to raise up a rival power, which, during two centuries, has thwarted the measures, opposed the arms, and checked the progress of his successors.

The next event of consequence in the fifteenth century, was the expedition of Charles VIII into Italy. This occasioned revolutions no less memorable; produced alterations, which were more immediatelly perceived, both in the military and political system; rouzed the states of Europe to bolder efforts; and blended their affairs and interests more closely together. The mild administration of Charles, a weak but generous Prince, seems to have revived the spirit and genius of the French nation, which the rigid despotism of his father had depressed, and almost extinguished. The ardour for military service, natural to the French nobility, returned, and their young monarch was impatient to distinguish his reign by some splendid enterprize. While he was uncertain towards what quarter he should turn his arms, the sollicitations and intrigues of an Italian politician, no less infamous on account of his crimes, than eminent for his abilities, determined his choice. Ludovico Sforza, having formed the design of deposing his nephew the duke of Milan, and of placing himself on the ducal throne, was so much afraid of a combination of the Italian powers to thwart this measure, and to support the injured Prince, with whom most of them were connected by blood or alliance, that he saw the necessity of securing the aid of some able protector. The King of France was the person to whom he applied; and without disclosing to him his own intentions, he laboured to prevail with him to march into Italy, at the head of a powerful army, in order to seize the crown of Naples, to which he had pretensions as heir to the house of Anjou. The right to that kingdom, claimed by the Angevin family, had been conveyed to Louis XI by Charles of Anjou, count of Maine and Provence. But that sagacious monarch, though he took immediate possession of those territories of which Charles was really master, totally disregarded his ideal title to a kingdom, over which another Prince reigned in tranquillity; and uniformly declined involving himself in the labyrinth of Italian politicks. His son, more adventurous, or more inconsiderate, embarked eagerly in this enterprize; and contemning all the remonstrances of his most experienced counsellors, prepared to carry it on with the utmost vigour.

Charles wanted not power equal to such a great undertaking. His father had transmitted to him such an ample prerogative, as gave him the entire command of his kingdom. He himself had added considerably to the extent of his dominions, by his prudent marriage with the heiress of Bretagne, which rendered him master of that province, the last of the great fiefs that remained to be annexed to the crown. He soon assembled forces which he thought sufficient; and so impatient was he to enter on his career as a conqueror, that sacrificing what was real, for what was chimerical, he restored Rousillon to Ferdinand, and gave up part of his father's acquisitions in Artois to Maximilian, with a view of inducing these Princes not to molest France, while he was carrying on his operations in Italy.

But so different were the efforts of the States of Europe in the fifteenth century, from those which we shall behold in the course of this history, that the army, with which Charles undertook this great enterprize, did not exceed twenty thousand men. The train of artillery, however, the ammunition, and warlike stores of every kind provided for its use, were so great as to bear some resemblance to the immense apparatus of modern war.[8]

When the French entered Italy, they met with nothing able to resist them. The Italian powers having remained, during a long period, undisturbed by the invasion of any foreign enemy, had formed a system with respect to their affairs, both in peace and war, peculiar to themselves. In order to adjust the interests, and balance the power of the different states into which Italy was divided, they were engaged in perpetual and endless negociations with each other, which they conducted with all the subtlety of a refining and deceitful policy. Their contests in the field, when they had recourse to arms, were decided in mock battles, by innocent and bloodless victories. Upon the first appearance of the danger which now impended, they had recourse to the arts which they had studied, and employed their utmost skill in intrigue in order to avert it. But this proving ineffectual, their effeminate mercenaries, the only military force that remained in the country, being fit only for the parade of service, were terrified at the aspect of real war, and shrunk at its approach. The impetuosity of the French valour appeared to them irresistible. Florence, Pisa, and Rome opened their gates as the French army advanced. The prospect of this dreadful invasion struck one King of Naples with such panic terror, that he died (if we may believe historians) of the fright. Another abdicated his throne from the same pusillanimous spirit. A third fled out of his dominions, as soon as the enemy appeared on the Neapolitan frontiers. Charles, after marching thither from the bottom of the Alps, with as much rapidity, and almost as little opposition, as if he had been on a progress through his own dominions, took quiet possession of the throne of Naples, and intimidated or gave law to every power in Italy.

Such was the conclusion of this expedition, which must be considered as the first great exertion of those new powers which the Princes of Europe had acquired, and now began to exercise. Its effects were no less considerable than its success had been astonishing. The Italians, unable to resist the impression of the enemy which broke in upon them, permitted him to hold on his course undisturbed. They quickly perceived that no single power, which they could rouze to action, was an equal match for a monarch, who ruled over such extensive territories, and was at the head of such a martial people; but that a confederacy might accomplish what the separate members of it durst not attempt. To this expedient, the only one that remained to deliver or to preserve them from the yoke, they had recourse. While Charles inconsiderately wasted his time at Naples, in festivals and triumphs on account of his past successes, or was fondly dreaming of future conquests in the East, to the empire of which he now aspired, they formed against him a powerful combination of almost all the Italian states, supported by the Emperor Maximilian, and Ferdinand King of Aragon. The union of so many powers, who suspended or forgot all their particular animosities, that they might act with concert against an enemy who had become formidable to them all, awakened Charles from his thoughtless security. He saw now no prospect of safety but in returning to France. An army of thirty thousand men, assembled by the allies, was ready to obstruct his march; and though the French, with a daring courage, which more than counterbalanced their inferiority in number, broke through that great body, and gained a victory, which opened to their monarch a safe passage into his own territories, he was stripped of all his conquests in Italy in as short a time as it had cost him to acquire them; and the political system in that country resumed the same appearance as before his invasion.

The sudden and decisive effect of this confederacy seems to have instructed the Princes and statesmen of Italy as much, as the irruption of the French had disconcerted and alarmed them. They had now extended to the affairs of Europe, the maxims of that political science which had hitherto been applied only to regulate the operations of the petty states in their own country. They had discovered the method of preventing any monarch from rising to such a degree of power, as was inconsistent with the general liberty; and had manifested the importance of attending to that great secret in modern policy, the preservation of a proper distribution of power among all the members of the system into which the states of Europe are formed. During all the wars of which Italy now became the theatre, and amidst the hostile operations which the imprudence of Louis XII and the ambition of Ferdinand of Aragon, carried on in that country, with little interruption, from the close of the fifteenth century, to that period at which the subsequent history commences, the maintaining a proper balance of power between the contending parties became the great object of attention to the statesmen of Italy. Nor was the idea confined to them. Self-preservation taught other powers to adopt it. It grew to be fashionable and universal. From this æra we can trace the progress of that intercourse between nations, which has linked the powers of Europe so closely together; and can discern the operations of that provident policy, which, during peace, guards against remote and contingent dangers; which, in war, hath prevented rapid and destructive conquests.

This was not the only effect of the operations which the great powers of Europe carried on in Italy. They contributed to render such a change, as the French had begun to make in the state of their troops, general; and obliged all the Princes, who appeared on this new theatre of action, to establish the military force of their kingdoms on the same footing with that of France. When the seat of war came to be remote from the countries which maintained the contest, the service of the feudal vassals ceased to be of any use; and the necessity of employing troops regularly trained to arms, and kept in constant pay, came at once to be evident. When Charles marched into Italy, his cavalry was entirely composed of those companies of Gendarmes, embodied by Charles VII and continued by Louis XI, his infantry consisted partly of Swiss, hired of the cantons, and partly of Gascons, armed and disciplined after the Swiss model. To these Louis XII added a body of Germans, well known in the wars of Italy by the name of the Black Bands. But neither of these monarchs made any account of the feudal militia, or ever had recourse to that military force which they might have commanded, in virtue of the ancient institutions in their kingdom. Maximilian and Ferdinand, as soon as they began to act in Italy, employed the same instruments, and trusted the execution of their plans entirely to mercenary troops.

This innovation in the military system was quickly followed by another, which the custom of employing Swiss in the Italian wars, was the occasion of introducing. The arms and discipline of the Swiss were different from those of other European nations. During their long and violent struggles in defence of their liberties against the house of Austria, whose armies, like those of other considerable Princes, consisted chiefly of heavy armed cavalry, the Swiss found that their poverty, and the small number of gentlemen residing in their country, at that time barren and uncultivated, put it out of their power to bring into the field any body of horse capable of facing the enemy. Necessity compelled them to place all their confidence in infantry; and in order to render it capable of withstanding the shock of cavalry, they gave the soldiers breast-plates and helmets as defensive armour; together with long spears, halberts, and heavy swords as weapons of offence. They formed them into large battalions, ranged in deep and close array, so as to present on every side a formidable front to the enemy.[9] The men at arms could make no impression on the solid strength of such body. It repulsed the Austrians in all their attempts to conquer Switzerland. It broke the Burgundian Gendarmerie, which was scarce inferior to that of France, either in number or reputation: And when first called to act in Italy, it bore down by its irresistible force every enemy that attempted to oppose it. These repeated proofs of the decisive effect of infantry, exhibited on such conspicuous occasions, restored that service to reputation, and gradually re-established the opinion, which had been long exploded, of its superior importance in the operations of war. But the glory which the Swiss had acquired, having inspired them with such high ideas of their own prowess and consequence, as rendered them mutinous and insolent, the Princes who employed them became weary of depending on the caprice of foreign mercenaries, and began to turn their attention towards the improvement of their national infantry.

The German powers having the command of men, whom nature has endowed with that steady courage, and persevering strength, which forms them to be soldiers, soon modelled their troops in such a manner, that they vied with the Swiss both in discipline and valour.

The French monarchs, though more slowly, and with greater difficulty, accustomed the impetuous spirit of their people to subordination and discipline; and were at such pains to render their national infantry respectable, that as early as the reign of Louis XII several gentlemen of high rank had so far abandoned their ancient ideas, as to condescend to enter into that service.[10]

The Spaniards, whose situation made it difficult to employ any other than their national troops, in the southern parts of Italy, which was the chief scene of their operations in that country, not only adopted the Swiss discipline, but improved upon it, by mingling a proper number of soldiers armed with heavy muskets in their battalions; and thus formed that famous body of infantry, which, during a century and a half, was the admiration and terror of all Europe. The Italian states gradually diminished the number of their cavalry, and, in imitation of their more powerful neighbours, brought the strength of their armies to consist in foot soldiers. From this period the nations of Europe have carried on war with forces more adapted to every species of service, more capable of acting in every country, and better fitted both for making conquests, and for preserving them.

As their efforts in Italy led the people of Europe to these improvements in the art of war, they gave them likewise the first idea of the expence which accompanies great and continued operations, and accustomed them to the burden of those impositions, which are necessary for supporting them. While the feudal policy subsisted in full vigour, while armies were composed of military vassals called forth to attack some neighbouring power, and to perform, in a short campaign, the services which they owed to their sovereign, the expence of war was extremely moderate. A small subsidy enabled a Prince to begin and to finish his greatest operations. But when Italy became the theatre on which the powers of Europe contended for superiority, the preparations requisite for such a distant expedition, the pay of armies kept constantly on foot, their subsistance in a foreign country, the sieges to be undertaken, and the towns to be defended, swelled the charges of war immensely, and by creating demands unknown in less active times, multiplied taxes in every kingdom. The progress of ambition, however, was so rapid, and Princes extended their operations so fast, that it was im-

possible at first to establish funds proportional to the increase
of expence which these occasioned. When Charles VIII invaded
Naples, the sums requisite for carrying on that enterprize so
far exceeded those which France had been accustomed to contribute, that before he reached the frontiers of Italy, his treasury
was exhausted, and the domestick resources, of which his extensive prerogative gave him the command, were at an end.
As he durst not venture to lay any new imposition on his people,
oppressed already with the weight of unusual burdens; the only
expedient that remained was, to borrow of the Genoese as much
money as would enable him to continue his march. But he could
not obtain the sum that was requisite, without consenting to pay
annually the exorbitant interest of forty-two livres for every hundred that he received.[11] We may observe the same disproportion
between the efforts and revenues of other Princes, his contemporaries. From this period, taxes went on increasing; and during
the reign of Charles V such sums were levied in every state, as
would have appeared prodigious at the close of the fifteenth
century, and gradually prepared the way for the more exorbitant exactions of modern times.

The last transaction, previous to the reign of Charles V that
merits attention on account of its influence upon the state of
Europe, is the league of Cambray. To humble the republick of
Venice, and to divide its territories, was the object of all the
powers who united in this confederacy. The civil constitution of
Venice, established on a firm basis, had suffered no considerable alteration for several centuries; during which, the state
conducted its affairs by maxims of policy no less prudent than
vigorous, and adhered to these, with an uniform consistent spirit,
which gave that commonwealth great advantage over other
states, whose views and measures changed as often as the form
of their government, or the persons who administered it. By
these unintermitted exertions of wisdom and valour, the Venetians enlarged the dominions of their commonwealth, until it
became the most considerable power in Italy. While their extensive commerce, the useful and curious manufactures which

they carried on, together with their monopoly of the precious commodities of the East, rendered Venice the most opulent state in Europe.

Their power was the object of terror to their Italian neighbours. Their wealth was viewed with envy by the greatest monarchs, who could not vie with their private citizens in the magnificence of their buildings, in the richness of their dress and furniture, or in splendor and elegance of living.[12] Julius II whose ambition was superior, and his abilities equal, to those of any Pontiff who ever sat on the Papal throne, formed the idea of this league against the Venetians, and endeavoured, by applying to these passions which I have mentioned, to persuade other Princes to join in it. By working upon the fears of the Italian powers, and upon the avarice of the monarchs beyond the Alps, he induced them, in concurrence with other causes, which it is not my province to explain, to form against these haughty republicans one of the most extensive confederacies Europe had ever beheld.

The Emperor, the King of France, the King of Aragon, the Pope, were principals in the league of Cambray, to which almost all the Princes of Italy acceded, the least considerable of them hoping for some share in the spoils of a state, which they already deemed to be devoted to destruction. The Venetians might have diverted this storm, or have broken its force; but with a presumptuous rashness, to which there is nothing similar in the course of their history, they waited its approach. The impetuous valour of the French rendered ineffectual all their precautions for the safety of the republick; and the fatal battle of Ghiarradadda entirely ruined the army, on which they relied for defence. Julius seized all the towns which they held in the ecclesiastical territories. Ferdinand re-annexed the towns of which they had got possession on the coast of Calabria, to his Neapolitan dominions. Maximilian, at the head of a powerful army, advanced towards Venice on the one side. The French pushed their conquests on the other. The Venetians, surrounded by so many enemies, and left without one ally, sunk from the height of presumption to the depths of despair; abandoned all their territories on the continent; and shut themselves up in their capital, as their last refuge, and the only place which they hoped to preserve.

This rapid success, however, proved fatal to the confederacy. The members of it, united while engaged in seizing their prey, began to feel their ancient jealousy and animosities revive, as soon as they had a prospect of dividing it. When the Venetians observed these symptoms of alienation and distrust, a ray of hope broke in upon them; the spirit natural to their councils returned; they resumed such wisdom and firmness, as made some atonement for their former imprudence and dejection; they recovered part of the territory which they had lost; they appeased the Pope and Ferdinand by well-timed concessions in their favour; and at length dissolved the confederacy, which had brought their commonwealth to the brink of ruin.

Julius, elated with beholding the effects of a league which he himself had planned, and imagining that nothing was too arduous for him to undertake, conceived the idea of expelling every foreign power out of Italy, and bent all the force of his mind towards executing a scheme so well suited to his vast and enterprizing genius. He directed his first attack against the French, who, on many accounts, were more odious to the Italians, than any of the foreigners who had acquired dominion in their country. By his activity and address, he prevailed on most of the powers, who had joined in the league of Cambray, to turn their arms against the King of France, their former ally; and engaged Henry VIII who had lately ascended the throne of England, to favour their operations by invading France. Louis XII resisted all the efforts of this formidable and unexpected confederacy, with undaunted fortitude. Hostilities were carried on, during several campaigns, in Italy, on the frontiers of Spain, and in Picardy, with alternate success. Exhausted at length, by the variety as well as extent of his operations; unable to withstand a confederacy which brought against him superior force, conducted with wisdom, and acting with perseverance; he found it necessary to conclude separate treaties of peace with his enemies; and the war terminated with the loss of every thing which the French had acquired in Italy, except the castle of Milan, and a few other inconsiderable towns in that dutchy.

The various negociations carried on during this busy period, and the different combinations formed among powers hitherto little connected with each other, greatly increased that intercourse between the nations of Europe, which I have mentioned as one effect of the events in the fifteenth century. While the greatness of the objects at which they aimed, the distant expeditions which they undertook, as well as the length and obstinacy of the contests in which they engaged, obliged them to exert themselves with a vigour and perseverance unknown in the preceeding ages.

Those active scenes which the following History will exhibit, and the variety and importance of those transactions which distinguish the period to which it extends, are not to be ascribed solely to the ambition, to the abilities, or to the rivalship of Charles V and of Francis I. The kingdoms of Europe had arrived at such a degree of improvement in the internal administration of government, and Princes had acquired such command of the national force which was to be exerted in foreign wars, that they were in a condition to enlarge the sphere of operations, and to increase the vigour of their efforts. Their contests in Italy, which led them first to try the extent of the power that they had acquired, gave rise to so many opposite claims and pretensions, excited such a spirit of discord and rivalship between nations, and laid the foundations of so many quarrels, as could not fail of producing extraordinary convulsions in Europe; and the sixteenth century opened with the certain prospect of its abounding in great and interesting events.

III

The Political Constitution of the Principal States in Europe at the Commencement of the Sixteenth Century

HAVING thus enumerated the principal causes and events, the influence of which extended to all the states in Europe, and contributed either to improve their internal government and police, or to enlarge the sphere of their activity, and to augment their national force; nothing remains, in order to prepare my readers for entering with full information upon perusing the History of the Reign of Charles V but to give some view of the particular constitution and form of civil government, in each of the nations which acted any considerable part during that period. While these institutions and occurrences, which I have mentioned, formed the people of Europe to resemble each other, and conducted them from barbarism to refinement, in the same path, and with almost equal steps, there were other circumstances which occasioned a difference in their political establishments, and gave rise to those peculiar modes of government, which have produced such variety in the character and genius of nations.

It is no less necessary to become acquainted with the latter, than to have contemplated the former. The view which I have exhibited of the causes and events, whose influence was universal will enable my readers to account for the surprizing resemblance among the nations of Europe in their interior police, and foreign operations. But, without a distinct knowledge of the peculiar form and genius of their civil government, a great part of their transactions must appear altogether mysterious and inexplicable. The historians of particular States, as they seldom extended their views farther than to the amusement or instruction of their fellow-citizens, by whom they might presume that all domestick customs and institutions were perfectly understood, have often neglected to descend into such details with respect to these, as are sufficient to convey to foreigners full light and information concerning the occurrences which they relate. But a history, which comprehends the transactions of so many different countries, would be extremely imperfect, without a previous survey of their constitution and political state. It is from his knowledge of these that the reader must draw those principles, which will enable him to judge with discernment, and to decide with certainty concerning the conduct of nations.

A minute detail, however, of the peculiar forms and regulations in every country, would lead to deductions of immeasurable length. To sketch out the great lines which distinguish and characterize each government, is all that the nature of my present work will admit of, and all that is necessary to illustrate the events which it records.

At the opening of the sixteenth century, the political face of Italy was extremely different from that of any other part of Europe. Instead of those extensive monarchies, which occupied the rest of the continent, that delightful country was parcelled out among many small states, each of which possessed sovereign and independant jurisdiction. The only monarchy in Italy was that of Naples. The dominion of the Popes was of a peculiar species, to which there is nothing similar either in ancient or modern times. In Venice and Florence, a republican form of government was established. Milan was subject to sovereigns, who had assumed no higher title than that of Dukes.

The Pope was the first of these powers in dignity, and not the least considerable by the extent of his territories. In the primitive church, the jurisdiction of bishops was equal and co-ordinate. They derived, perhaps, some degree of consideration from the dignity of the See in which they presided. They possessed, however, no real authority or pre-eminence, but what they acquired by superior abilities, or superior sanctity. As Rome had so long been the seat of Empire, and capital of the world, its bishops were on that account entitled to respect; they received it; but during several ages they claimed and received nothing more. From these humble beginnings, they advanced with such an adventurous and well-directed ambition, that they established a spiritual dominion over the minds and sentiments of men, to which all Europe submitted with implicit obedience. Their claim of universal jurisdiction, as heads of the church, and their pretensions to infallibility in their decisions, as successors of St. Peter, are as chimerical, as they are repugnant to the genius of the Christian religion. But on these foundations, the superstition and credulity of mankind enabled them to erect an amazing superstructure. In all ecclesiastical controversies, their decisions were received as the infallible oracles of truth. Nor was the plenitude of their power confined to these alone; they dethroned monarchs; disposed of crowns; absolved subjects from the obedience due to their sovereigns; and laid kingdoms under interdicts. There was not a state in Europe which had not been disquieted by their ambition. There was not a throne which they had not shaken; nor a Prince, who did not tremble at their power.

Nothing was wanting to render this Empire absolute, and to establish it on the ruins of all civil authority, but that the Popes should have possessed such a degree of temporal power, as was sufficient to second and enforce their spiritual decrees. Happily for mankind, while their spiritual jurisdiction was most extensive, and at its greatest height, their temporal property was extremely limited. They were powerful Pontiffs, formidable at a distance; but they were petty Princes, without any considerable domestick force. They had early endeavoured, indeed, to acquire territory by arts, similar to those which they had employed in extending their jurisdiction. Under pretence of a donation from

Constantine, and of another from Charlemagne or his father Pepin, they attempted to take possession of some towns adjacent to Rome. But these donations were fictitious, and availed them little. The benefactions, for which they were indebted to the credulity of the Norman adventurers, who conquered Naples, and to the superstition of the countess Matilda, were real, and added ample domains to the Holy See.

But the power of the Popes did not increase in proportion to the extent of territory which they had acquired. In the dominions annexed to the Holy See, as well as in those subject to other Princes in Italy, the sovereign of a state was far from having the command of the force which it contained. During the turbulence and confusion of the middle ages, the powerful nobility or leaders of popular factions in Italy, had seized the government of different towns; and after strengthening their fortifications, and taking a body of mercenaries into pay, they set up for independance. The territory which the church had gained, was filled with such petty tyrants, who left the Pope hardly the shadow of dominion.

As these usurpations almost annihilated the Papal power in the greater part of the towns subject to the church, the Roman barons frequently disputed the authority of the Popes, even in Rome itself. In the twelfth century, an opinion began to be propagated, "That as the function of ecclesiastics was purely spiritual, they ought to possess no property, and to claim no temporal jurisdiction; but, according to the laudable example of their predecessors in the primitive church, should subsist wholly upon their tithes, or upon the voluntary oblations of the people."[1] This doctrine being addressed to men, who had beheld the scandalous manner in which the avarice and ambition of the clergy had prompted them to contend for wealth, and to exercise power, they listened to it with fond attention. The Roman barons, who had felt most sensibly the rigour of ecclesiastical oppression, adopted these sentiments with such ardour, that they set themselves instantly to shake off the yoke. They endeavoured to restore some image of their ancient liberty, by reviving the institution of the Roman senate, in which they vested supreme

100

authority; committing the executive power sometimes to one chief senator, sometimes to two, and sometimes to a magistrate dignified with the name of *The Patrician*. The Popes exerted themselves with vigour, in order to check this fatal encroachment on their jurisdiction. One of them, finding all his endeavours ineffectual, was so much mortified, that extreme grief cut short his days. Another, having ventured to attack the senators at the head of some armed men, was mortally wounded in the fray.[2] During a considerable period, the power of the Popes, before which the greatest monarchs in Europe trembled, was circumscribed within such narrow limits in their own capital, that they durst scarce exert any act of authority without the permission and concurrence of the senate.

Encroachments were made upon the Papal authority, not only by the usurpations of the Roman nobility, but by the mutinous spirit of the people. During seventy years of the fourteenth century, the Popes fixed their residence in Avignon. The inhabitants of Rome, accustomed to consider themselves as the descendants of the people who had conquered the world, and had given laws to it, were too high-spirited to submit with patience to the delegated authority of those persons, to whom the Popes committed the government of the city. On many occasions, they opposed the execution of the Papal mandates, and on the slightest appearance of innovation or oppression, they were ready to take arms in defence of their own immunities. Towards the middle of the fourteenth century, being instigated by Nicolas Rienzo, a man of low birth and a seditious spirit, but of popular eloquence, and an enterprizing ambition, they drove all the nobility out of the city, established a democratical form of government, elected Rienzo Tribune of the people, and invested him with extensive authority. But though the frantick proceedings of the tribune soon overturned this new system; though the government of Rome was reinstated in its ancient form; yet every fresh attack contributed to weaken the papal jurisdiction; and the turbulence of the people concurred with the spirit of independance among the nobility, to circumscribe it within very narrow bounds.[3] Gregory VII and other domineering Pontiffs, accomplished those great things which rendered them so formidable to the Emperors with whom they contended, not by the force of their arms, or by the extent of their power, but by the dread of their spiritual censures, and by the effect of their intrigues, which excited rivals, and called forth enemies against every Prince, whom they wished to depress or to destroy.

Many attempts were made by the Popes, not only to humble these usurpers, who lorded it over the cities in the ecclesiastical state, but to break the turbulent spirit of the Roman people. These were long unsuccessful. At last Alexander VI with a policy no less artful than flagitious, subdued and extirpated most of them, and rendered the Popes masters of their own dominions. The enterprizing ambition of Julius II added conquests of no inconsiderable value to the patrimony of St. Peter. Thus the Popes, by degrees, became powerful temporal Princes. Their territories, in the age of Charles V were of greater extent than at present; their country was better cultivated, and more populous; and as they drew large contributions from every part of Europe, their revenues far exceeded those of the neighbouring powers, and rendered them capable of more sudden and vigorous efforts.

The genius of the Papal government, however, was better adapted to the exercise of spiritual dominion, than of temporal power. With respect to the former, all its maxims were steady and invariable. Every new Pontiff adopted the plan of his predecessor. By education and habit Ecclesiastics were so formed, that the character of the individual was sunk in that of the profession; and the passions of the man were sacrificed to the interest and honour of the order. The hands which held the reins of administration might change; but the spirit which conducted them was always the same. While the measures of other governments fluctuated, and the objects at which they aimed varied, the church kept one end in view; and to this unrelaxing constancy of pursuit, it was indebted for its success in the boldest attempts ever made by human ambition.

But in their civil administration, the Popes followed no such uniform or consistent plan. There, as in other governments, the character, the passions, and the interests of the person who had the supreme direction of affairs, occasioned a variation both in objects and measures. As few Prelates reached the summit of ecclesiastical dignity, until they were far advanced in life, a change of masters was more frequent in the Papal dominions than in other states, and the political system was, of course, less stable and permanent. Every Pope was eager to make the most of the short period, during which he had the prospect of enjoying power, in order to aggrandize his family, and to attain his private ends; and it was often the first business of his successor to undo all that he had done, and to overturn what he had established.

As ecclesiasticks were trained to pacifick arts, and early initiated in the mysteries of that policy, by which the court of Rome extended or supported its spiritual dominion, the Popes were apt to conduct their temporal affairs with the same spirit; and in all their measures were more ready to employ the refinements of intrigue, than the force of arms. It was in the Papal court that address and subtlety in negociation first became a science; and during the sixteenth century, Rome was considered as the school in which it could be best acquired.

As the decorum of their ecclesiastical character prevented the Popes from placing themselves at the head of their armies, or taking the command, in person, of the military force in their dominions, they were afraid to arm their subjects; and in all their operations, whether offensive or defensive, they trusted entirely to mercenary troops.

As their power and dominions could not descend to their posterity, the Popes were less sollicitous than other Princes to form or to encourage schemes of publick utility and improvement. Their tenure was only for a short life; present advantage was all that they attended to; to squeeze and to amass, not to meliorate, was their object. They erected, perhaps, some work of ostentation, to remain as a monument of their Pontificate; they found it necessary, at some times, to establish useful institutions, in order to sooth and silence the turbulent populace of Rome; but plans of general benefit to their subjects, and framed with a view to futurity, were rarely objects of attention in the

Papal policy. The patrimony of St. Peter was worse governed than any part of Europe; and though a generous Pontiff might suspend for a little, or counter-act the effects of those vices which are peculiar to the administration of ecclesiasticks; the disease not only remained incurable, but has even gone on increasing from age to age; and the decline of the state has kept pace with its progress.

One circumstance, farther, concerning the Papal government, is so singular, as to merit attention. As the spiritual supremacy and temporal power were united in one person, and uniformly aided each other in their operations, they became so blended together, that it was difficult to separate them, even in imagination. The potentates who found it necessary to oppose the measures which the Popes pursued as temporal Princes, could not divest themselves of the reverence which they imagined to be due to them as heads of the church, and vicars of Jesus Christ. It was with reluctance that they could be brought to a rupture with them; they were averse to push their operations against them to extremity; they listened eagerly to the first overtures of accommodation, and were willing to procure it almost upon any terms. Their consciousness of this encouraged the enterprizing Pontiffs, who filled the Papal throne about the beginning of the sixteenth century, to engage in schemes seemingly the most extravagant. They trusted, that if their temporal power was not sufficient to carry them through with success, the respect paid to their spiritual dignity would enable them to extricate themselves with facility and with honour. But when Popes came to take part more frequently in the contests among Princes, and to engage as principals or auxiliaries in every war kindled in Europe, this veneration for their sacred character began to abate; and striking instances will occur in the following history, of its being almost totally extinct.

Of all the Italian powers, the republick of Venice, next to the Pope, was most connected with the rest of Europe. The rise of that commonwealth, during the inroads of the Huns in the fifth century; the singular situation of its capital in the small isles of the Adriatick gulf; and the more singular form of its civil constitution, are generally known. If we view the Venetian government as calculated for the order of the nobles alone, its institutions are so excellent; the deliberative, legislative and executive powers are so admirably distributed and adjusted, that it must be regarded as a perfect model of political wisdom. But if we consider it as formed for a numerous body of people subject to its jurisdiction, it will appear a rigid and partial aristocracy, which lodges all power in the hands of a few members of the community, while it degrades and oppresses the rest.

The spirit of government, in a commonwealth of this species, was, of course, timid and jealous. The Venetian nobles distrusted their own subjects, and were afraid of allowing them the use of arms. They encouraged among them the arts of industry and commerce; they employed them in manufactures and in navigation; but never admitted them into the troops which the state kept in its pay. The military force of the republick consisted entirely of foreign mercenaries. The command of these was never trusted to noble Venetians, lest they should acquire such influence over the army, as might endanger the publick liberty; or become accustomed to the exercise of such power, as would make them unwilling to return to the condition of private citizens. A soldier of fortune was placed at the head of the armies of the commonwealth; and to obtain that honour, was the great object of the Italian *Condottieri,* or leaders of bands, who, in the fifteenth and sixteenth centuries, made a trade of war, and raised and hired out soldiers to different states. But the same suspicious policy, which induced them to employ these adventurers, prevented their placing entire confidence in them. Two noblemen, appointed by the senate, accompanied their army when it took the field, with the appellation of *Proveditori,* and like the field-deputies of the Dutch republick in later times, observed all the motions of the general, and checked and controuled him in all his operations.

A republick, with such civil and military institutions, was not formed to make conquests. While its subjects were disarmed, and its nobles excluded from military command, it carried on its warlike enterprizes with great disadvantage. This ought to have taught the Venetians to make self-preservation, and the enjoyment of domestick security, the objects of their policy. But republicks are apt to be seduced by the spirit of ambition, as well as Princes. When the Venetians so far forgot the interior defects in their government, as to aim at extensive conquests, the fatal blow, which they received in the war excited by the league of Cambray, convinced them of the imprudence and danger of making violent efforts, in opposition to the genius and tendency of their constitution.

It is not, however, by its military, but by its naval and commercial power, that the importance of the Venetian commonwealth must be estimated. In the latter, the real force and nerves of the state consisted. The jealousy of government did not extend to this department. Nothing was apprehended from this quarter, that could prove formidable to liberty. The senate encouraged the nobles to trade, and to serve on board the fleet. They became merchants and admirals. They increased the wealth of their country by their industry. They added to its dominions, by the valour with which they conducted its naval armaments.

The Venetian commerce was an inexhaustible source of opulence. All the nations in Europe depended upon them, not only for the commodities of the East, but for various manufactures fabricated by them alone, or finished with a dexterity and elegance unknown in other countries. From this extensive commerce, the state derived such immense supplies, as concealed these vices in its constitution, which I have mentioned; and enabled it to keep on foot such armies, as were not only an over-match for the force which any of its neighbours could bring into the field, but were sufficient to contend, for some time, with the powerful monarchs beyond the Alps. During its struggles with the Princes united against it by the league of Cambray, the republick levied sums which, even in the present age, would be deemed considerable; and while the King of France paid the exorbitant interest which I have mentioned for the money advanced to him, and the Emperor eager to borrow, but destitute of credit, was known by the name of *Maximilian the Money-less*, the Venetians raised whatever sums they pleased, at the moderate premium of five in the hundred.[4]

The constitution of Florence was perfectly the reverse of that of Venice. It partook as much of the democratical turbulence and licentiousness, as the other aristocratical rigour. Florence, however, was a commercial, not a military democracy. The nature of its institutions were favourable to commerce, and the genius of the people was turned towards it. The vast wealth which the family of Medici had acquired by trade; added to the magnificence, the generosity, and the virtue of the first Cosmo, gave him such an ascendant over the affections as well as the councils of his countrymen, that though the forms of popular government were preserved, though the various departments of administration were filled by magistrates distinguished by the ancient names, and elected in the usual manner, he was in reality the head of the commonwealth, and in the station of a private citizen he possessed supreme authority. Cosmo transmitted a considerable degree of this power to his descendants; and during the greater part of the fifteenth century, the political state of Florence was extremely singular. The appearance of republican government subsisted, the people were passionately attached to it, and on some occasions contended warmly for their privileges, and yet they permitted a single family to assume a direction of their affairs, almost as absolute as if it had been formally invested with sovereign power. The jealousy of the Medici concurred with the commercial spirit of the Florentines, in putting the military force of the republick upon the same footing with that of the other Italian states. The troops, which the Florentines employed in their wars, consisted almost entirely of mercenary soldiers, furnished by the *Condottieri*, or leaders of bands, whom they took into their pay.

In the kingdom of Naples, to which the sovereignty of the island of Sicily was annexed, the feudal government was established in the same form, and with the same defects, as in the other nations of Europe. The frequent and violent revolutions which happened in that monarchy, had considerably increased these defects, and rendered them more intolerable. The succession to the crown of Naples had been so often interrupted or altered, and so many Princes of foreign blood had taken possession of the throne, that the Neapolitan nobility had lost, in a great measure, that attachment to the family of their sovereigns, as well as that reverence for their persons, which, in other feudal kingdoms, contributed to set some bounds to the encroachments of the barons upon the royal prerogatives and power. At the same time, the different pretenders to the crown, being obliged to court the barons who adhered to them, and on whose support they depended for the success of their claims, they augmented their privileges by liberal concessions, and connived at their boldest usurpations. Even when seated on the throne, it was dangerous for a Prince, who held his sceptre by a disputed title, to venture on any step towards extending his own power, or circumscribing that of the nobles.

From all these causes, the kingdom of Naples was the most turbulent of any in Europe, and the authority of its Monarchs the least extensive. Though Ferdinand I who began his reign in the year one thousand four hundred and sixty-eight, attempted to break the power of the aristocracy; though his son Alfonso, that he might crush it at once by cutting off the leaders of greatest reputation and influence among the Neapolitan barons, venture to commit one of the most perfidious and cruel actions recorded in history; the order of nobles was nevertheless more exasperated than humbled by the blow.[5] The resentment which these outrages excited was so violent, and the power of the malecontent nobles was still so formidable, that to these may be ascribed, in a great degree, the ease and rapidity with which Charles VIII conquered the kingdom of Naples.[6]

The event that gave rise to the violent contests concerning the succession to the crown of Naples and Sicily, which brought so many calamities upon these kingdoms, happened in the thirteenth century. Upon the death of the Emperor Frederick II, Manfred his natural son aspiring to the Neapolitan throne, murdered (if we may believe contemporary historians) his brother the Emperor Conrad, and by that crime obtained possession of it.[7] The Popes, from their implacable enmity to the house of Swabia, not only refused to recognize Manfred's title, but endeavoured to excite against him some rival capable of wresting the sceptre out of his hand. Charles Count of Anjou, the brother of St. Louis King of France, undertook this; and he received from the Popes, the investiture of the kingdom of Naples and Sicily as a fief held of the Holy See. The Count of Anjou's efforts were crowned with success; Manfred fell in battle; and he took possession of the vacant throne. But soon after, Charles sullied the glory which he had acquired, by the injustice and cruelty with which he put to death, by the hands of the executioner, Conradin, the last Prince of the house of Swabia, and the rightful heir of the Neapolitan crown. That gallant young Prince asserted his title, to the last, with a courage, worthy of a better fate. On the scaffold, he declared Peter, at that time Prince, and soon after King of Aragon, who had married Manfred's only daughter, his heir; and throwing his glove among the people, he entreated that it might be carried to Peter as the symbol by which he conveyed all his rights to him.[8] The desire of avenging the insult offered to royalty by the death of Conradin concurred with ambition, in prompting Peter to take arms in support of the title, which he had acquired. From that period, during almost two centuries, the houses of Aragon and Anjou contended for the crown of Naples. Amidst a succession of revolutions more rapid, as well as of crimes more atrocious, than what occur in the history of almost any other kingdom, Monarchs sometimes of the Aragonese line, and sometimes of the Angevin were seated on the throne. At length the Princes of the house of Aragon obtained such firm possession of this long-disputed inheritance, that they transmitted it quietly to a bastard branch of their family.[9]

The race of the Angevin Kings, however, was not extinct; nor had they relinquished their title to the Neapolitan crown. The Count of Maine and Provence, the heir of this family, conveyed all his rights and pretensions to Louis XI and to his successors. Charles VIII, as I have already related, crossed the Alps at the head of a powerful army in order to prosecute his claim with a degree of vigour far superior to that, which the Princes from whom he derived it, had been capable of exerting. The rapid progress of his arms in Italy, as well as the short time during which he enjoyed the fruits of his success, are well known. Frederick the heir of the illegitimate branch of the Aragonese family, soon recovered the throne of which Charles had dispossessed him. Louis XII and Ferdinand of Aragon united against this Prince, whom both, though for different reasons, considered as an usurper, and agreed to divide his dominions between them. Frederick, unable to resist the combined Monarchs, each of whom was far his superior in power, resigned his sceptre. Louis and Ferdinand, though they had concurred in making the conquest, differed about the division of it; and from allies became enemies. But Gonsalvo de Cordova, partly by the exertion of such military talents as gave him a just title to the appellation of the *Great Captain,* which the Spanish historians have bestowed upon him; and partly by such shameless and frequent violations of the most solemn engagements, as leave an indelible stain on his memory; stripped the French of all that they possessed in the Neapolitan dominions, and secured the peaceable possession of them to his master. These, together with his other kingdoms, Ferdinand transmitted to his grandson Charles V, whose right to possess them, if not altogether uncontravertible, seems, at least, to be as well founded as that, which the Kings of France set in opposition to it.[10]

There is nothing in the political constitution, or interior government of the dutchy of Milan so remarkable, as to require a particular explanation. But as the right of succession to that fertile province was the cause or the pretext of almost all the wars carried on in Italy during the reign of Charles V, it is necessary to trace these disputes to their source, and to inquire into the pretensions of the various competitors.

During the long and fierce contests excited in Italy by the violence of the Guelf and Ghibelline factions, the family of Visconti rose to great eminence among their fellow-citizens of Milan. As the Visconti had adhered uniformly to the Ghibelline or Imperial interest, they by way of recompence, received, from one Emperor, the dignity of perpetual vicars of the Empire in Italy.[11] They were created by another, Dukes of Milan, and together with that title, the possession of the city and its territories, was bestowed upon them as an hereditary fief.[12] John King of France, among other expedients for raising money, which the calamities of his reign obliged him to employ, condescended to give one of his daughters in marriage to John Galeazzo Visconti the first Duke of Milan, from whom he had received considerable sums. Valentine Visconti one of the children of this marriage married her cousin, Louis Duke of Orleans, the only brother of Charles VI. In their marriage-contract which the Pope confirmed, it was stipulated that, upon failure of heirs-male in the family of Visconti, the dutchy of Milan should descend to the posterity of Valentine and the Duke of Orleans. That event took place. In the year one thousand four hundred and forty-seven, Philip Maria the last Prince of the ducal family of Visconti died. Various competitors pretended to the succession. Charles Duke of Orleans pleaded his right to it, founded on the marriage-contract of his mother Valentine Visconti. Alfonso King of Naples claimed it in consequence of a will made by Philip Maria in his favour. The Emperor contended that upon the extinction of male issue in the family of Visconti the fief returned to the superior Lord, and ought to be re-annexed to the Empire. The people of Milan smitten with that love of liberty which prevailed among the Italian States, declared against the dominion of any master, and established a republican form of government.

But during the struggle among so many competitors, the prize for which they contended was seized by one from whom none of them apprehended any danger. Francis Sforza, the natural son of Jacomuzzo Sforza, whom his courage and abilities had elevated from the rank of a peasant to be one of the most eminent and powerful of the Italian *Condottieri*, having succeeded his father in the command of the adventurers who followed his standard, had married a natural daughter of the last Duke of Milan. Upon this shadow of a title Francis founded his pretensions to the dutchy, which he supported with such talents and valour as placed him at last on the ducal throne. The virtues as well as abilities with which he governed, inducing his subjects to forget the defects in his title, he transmitted his dominions quietly to his son; from whom they descended to his grandson. He was murdered by his grand uncle Ludovico, surnamed the Moor, who took possession of the dutchy; and his right to it was confirmed by the investiture of the Emperor Maximilian in the year one thousand four hundred and ninety-four.[13]

Louis XI who took pleasure in depressing the Princes of the blood, and who admired the political abilities of Francis Sforza, would not permit the Duke of Orleans to take any step in prosecution of his right to the dutchy of Milan. Ludovico the Moor kept up such a close connection with Charles VIII that during the greater part of his reign, the claim of the family of Orleans continued to lie dormant. But when the crown of France devolved to Louis XII Duke of Orleans, he instantly asserted the rights of his family with the ardour which it was natural to expect. Ludovico Sforza, incapable of contending with such a rival, was stripped of all his dominions in the space of a few days. The King, clad in the ducal robes, entered Milan in triumph; and soon after, Ludovico having been betrayed by the Swiss in his pay, was sent a prisoner into France, and shut up in the castle of Loches, where he lay unpitied during the remainder of his days. In consequence of one of the singular revolutions which occur so frequently in the history of the Milanese, his son Maximilian Sforza was placed on the ducal throne, of which he kept possession during the reign of Louis XII. His successor Francis I was too high-spirited and enterprizing tamely to relinquish his title. As soon as he was seated upon the throne, he prepared to invade the Milanese; and his right of succession to it, appears from this detail, to have been not only more natural but more just than that of any other competitor.

It is unnecessary to enter into any detail with respect to the form of government in Genoa, Parma, Modena, and the other inferior States of Italy. Their names, indeed, will often occur in the following history. But the power of these States themselves was so inconsiderable, that their fate depended little upon their own efforts; and the frequent revolutions which they underwent, were brought about by the operations of the Princes who attacked or defended them, rather than by any thing peculiar in their internal constitution.

Of the great kingdoms on this side of the Alps, Spain is one of the most considerable; and it was the hereditary domain of

Charles V, as well as the chief source of his power and wealth, a distinct knowledge of its political constitution is of capital importance towards understanding the transactions of his reign.

The Vandals and Goths, who overturned the Roman power in Spain, established a form of government in that country, and brought in customs and laws, perfectly familiar to those which were introduced into the rest of Europe, by the other victorious tribes which acquired settlements there. For some time, society advanced, among the new inhabitants of Spain, by the same steps, and seemed to hold the same course, as in other European nations. To this progress, a sudden stop was put by the invasion of the Saracens or Moors. The Goths could not withstand the efforts of their enthusiastick valour, which subdued Spain, with the same impetuous rapidity that distinguishes all the operations of their arms. The conquerors introduced into the country in which they settled the Mahometan religion, the Arabick language, the manners of the East, together with that taste for the arts, and that love of elegance and splendour, which the Caliphs had begun to cultivate among their subjects.

Such Gothick nobles, as disdained to submit to the Moorish yoke, fled for refuge to the inaccessible mountains of Asturias, and comforted themselves with enjoying there the exercise of the Christian religion, and with maintaining the authority of their ancient laws. Being joined by many of the boldest and most warlike among their countrymen, they sallied out upon the adjacent settlements of the Moors, in small parties; and making short excursions, were satisfied with plunder and revenge, without thinking of conquest. By degrees, their strength increased, their views enlarged, a regular government was established among them, and they began to aim at extending their territories. While they pushed on their attacks with the unremitting ardour excited by zeal for religion, by the desire of vengeance, and by the hope of rescuing their country from oppression; while they conducted their operations with the courage natural to men who had no other occupation but war, and who were strangers to all the arts which corrupt or enfeeble the mind, the Moors gradually lost many of the advantages, to which

113

they had been indebted for their first success. They threw off all
dependance on the Caliphs;[14] they neglected to preserve a close
connection with their countrymen in Africa; their Empire in
Spain was split into many small kingdoms; together with the arts
which they cultivated, the luxury to which these gave rise, relaxed, in some measure, the force of their military institutions,
and abated the vigour of their war-like spirit. The Moors, however, continued still to be a gallant people, and possessed great
resources. According to the magnificent stile of the Spanish historians, eight centuries of almost uninterrupted war elapsed, and
three thousand seven hundred battles were fought before the
last of the Moorish kingdoms in Spain submitted to the Christian
arms.

As the Christians made their conquests upon the Mahometans
at various periods, and under different leaders, each formed the
territory which he had wrested from the common enemy, into an
independant State. Spain was divided into as many separate
kingdoms, as it contained provinces, and in each city of note, a
petty Monarch established his throne, and assumed all the ensigns of royalty. In a series of years, however, by the usual events
of intermarriages, or legal succession, or conquest, all these
inferior principalities were annexed to the more powerful kingdoms of Castile and of Aragon; and at length by the fortunate
marriage of Ferdinand and Isabella, the former the hereditary
Monarch of Aragon, and the latter raised to the throne of Castile
by the affection of her subjects, all the Spanish crowns were
united, and descended in the same line.

From this period, the political constitution of Spain began
to assume a regular and uniform appearance; the genius of government may be delineated, and the progress of its laws and
manners may be traced with certainty. Notwithstanding the singular revolution which had happened in Spain, and the peculiarity of its fate, in being so long subjected to the Mahometan yoke,
the customs introduced by the Vandals and Goths had taken
such deep root, and were so thoroughly incorporated with the
frame of its government, that in every province which the Christians recovered from the Moors, we find the condition of indi-

114

viduals, as well as the political constitution, nearly the same as in other nations of Europe. Lands were held by the same tenure; justice was dispensed in the same form; the same privileges were claimed by the nobility; and the same power exercised by the Cortes, or general assembly of the kingdom. Several circumstances contributed to secure this permanence of the feudal institutions in Spain, notwithstanding the conquest of the Moors, which seemed to have overturned them. Such of the Spaniards, as preserved their independance, adhered to their ancient customs not only from attachment to them, but out of antipathy to the Moors, to whose ideas concerning property and government these customs were so totally repugnant. Even among the Christians, who submitted to the Moorish conquerors, and consented to become their subjects, ancient customs were not entirely abolished. They were permitted to retain their religion; their laws concerning private property; their forms of administering justice; and their mode of levying taxes. The followers of Mahomet are the only enthusiasts, who have united the spirit of toleration with zeal for making proselytes, and who, at the same time that they took arms to propagate the doctrine of their prophet, permitted such as would not embrace it, to adhere to their own tenets and to practice their own rites. To this peculiarity in the genius of the Mahometan religion, as well as to the desire of the Moors to reconcile the Christians to their yoke, it was owing that the ancient manners and laws in Spain survived the violent shock of a conquest, and continued to subsist, notwithstanding the introduction of a new religion and a new form of government into that country. It is obvious from all these particulars, that the Christians must have found it extremely easy to re-establish manners and government on their ancient foundations, in those provinces of Spain, which they wrested successively from the Moors. A considerable part of the people retained such a fondness for the customs, and such a reverence for the laws of their ancestors, that they wished to see them restored with full authority, and were not only willing but eager to observe the former, and to recognize the authority of the latter.

But though the feudal form of government, with all the

institutions that characterize it, was thus preserved entire in Castile and Aragon, as well as in all the kingdoms which depended on these crowns, there were certain peculiarities in their political constitutions which distinguish them from those of any other country in Europe. The regal prerogative, extremely limited in every feudal kingdom, was circumscribed, in Spain, within such narrow bounds, as reduced the power of the sovereign almost to nothing. The privileges of the nobility were vast in proportion, and extended so far, as to border on absolute independance. The immunities of the cities were great, they possessed considerable influence in the Cortes or supreme assemblies of the nations, and they aspired at obtaining more. Such a state of society, in which the political machine was so ill adjusted, and the several members of the legislature so improperly balanced, produced interior disorders in the kingdoms of Spain, which rose beyond the pitch of turbulence and anarchy, usual under the feudal government. The whole tenor of the Spanish history confirms the truth of this observation; and when the mutinous spirit, to which the genius of their policy gave birth and vigour, was not restrained and overawed by the immediate dread of the Moorish arms, it broke out into more frequent insurrections against the government of their Princes, as well as more outrageous insults on their dignity, than occur in the annals of any other country. These were accompanied at some times with more liberal sentiments concerning the rights of the people, at other times with more elevated notions concerning the privileges of the nobles, than were common in other nations.

In the principality of Catalonia, which was annexed to the kingdom of Aragon, the impatience of the people to obtain the redress of their grievances having prompted them to take arms against their sovereign John II, they, by a solemn deed, recalled the oath of allegiance which they had sworn to him, declared him and his posterity to be unworthy of the throne,[15] and endeavoured to establish a republican form of government, in order to secure the perpetual enjoyment of that liberty, after which they aspired.[16] Nearly about the same period, the indignation of the Castilian nobility against the weak and flagitious administration of Henry IV, having led them to combine against him, they arrogated as one of the privileges belonging to their order, the right of trying and of passing sentences on their sovereign. That the exercise of this power might be as publick and solemn, as the pretension to it was bold, they summoned all the nobility of their party to meet at Avila, a spacious theatre was erected in a plain without the walls of the town, an image representing the King, was seated on a throne, clad in royal robes, with a crown on its head, a sceptre in its hand, and the sword of justice by its side. The accusation against the King was read, and the sentence of deposition was pronounced, in presence of a numerous assembly. At the close of the first article of the charge, the archbishop of Toledo advanced, and tore the crown from the head of the image; at the close of the second, the Conde de Placentia snatched the sword of justice from its side; at the close of the third, the Conde de Benevente wrested the sceptre from its hand; at the close of the last, Don Diego Lopes de Stuniga tumbled it headlong from the throne. At the same instant, Don Alfonso, Henry's brother, was proclaimed King of Castile and Leon in his stead.[17]

The most daring leaders of faction would not have ventured on these measures, nor have conducted them with such publick ceremony, if the sentiments of the people concerning the royal dignity, had not been so formed by the laws and policy, to which they were accustomed both in Castile and Aragon, as prepared them to approve of such extraordinary proceedings, or to acquiesce in them.

In Aragon, the form of government was monarchical, but the genius and maxims of it were purely republican. The Kings, who were long elective, retained only the shadow of power; the real exercise of it was in the Cortes or parliament of the kingdom. This supreme assembly was composed of four different *arms* or members. The nobility of the first rank. The Equestrian order, or nobility of the second class. The representatives of the cities and towns, whose right to a place in the Cortes, if we may give credit to the historians of Aragon, was coeval with the constitution. The ecclesiastical order, composed of the dignitaries of the church, together with the representatives of the inferior clergy.[18] No law could pass in this assembly without the assent of every single member who had a right to vote.[19] Without the permission of the Cortes, no tax could be imposed; no war could be declared; no peace concluded; no money could be coined; nor any alteration be made in the current specie.[20] The power of reviewing the proceedings of all inferior courts, the privilege of inspecting every department of administration, and the right of redressing all grievances belonged to the Cortes. Nor did those who conceived themselves to be aggrieved address the Cortes in the humble tone of supplicants, and petition for redress; they demanded it as the birth-right of free men, and required the guardians of their liberty to decide with respect to the points which they laid before them.[21] This sovereign court was held, during several centuries, every year; but, in consequence of a regulation introduced about the beginning of the fourteenth century, it was convened from that period only once in two years. After it was assembled, the King had no right to prorogue or dissolve it without its own consent; and the session continued forty days.[22]

Not satisfied with having erected these barriers against the encroachments of the royal prerogative, nor willing to rely for the preservation of their liberties on the vigilance and authority of an assembly, similar to the diets, states general, and parliaments, in which the other feudal nations placed so much confidence, the Aragonese had recourse to an institution peculiar to themselves, and elected a *Justiza* or supreme judge. This magistrate, whose office bore some resemblance to that of the Ephori in ancient Sparta, acted as the guardian of the people, and the comptroller of the Prince. The person of the Justiza was sacred, and his power and jurisdiction almost unbounded. He was the supreme interpreter of the laws. Not only inferior judges, but the Kings themselves were bound to consult him in every doubtful case, and to receive his responses with implicit deference.[23] An appeal lay to him from the royal judges, as well as from those appointed by the barons within their respective territories. Even when no appeal was made to him, he could interpose by his own authority, prohibit the ordinary judge to proceed, take immediate cognizance of the cause himself, and remove the party accused to the *Manifestation* or prison of the state, to which no person had access but by his permission. His power was exerted with no less vigour and effect in superintending the administration of government, than in regulating the course of justice. It was the prerogative of the Justiza to inspect the conduct of the King. He had a title to review all the royal proclamations and patents, and to declare whether or not they were agreeable to law, and ought to be carried into execution. He, by his sole authority, could exclude any of the King's ministers from the conduct of affairs, and call them to answer for their mal-administration. He himself was accountable to the Cortes alone, for the manner in which he discharged the duties of this high office, and performed functions of the greatest importance that could be committed to a subject.[24]

It is evident from a bare enumeration of the privileges of the Aragonese Cortes, as well as of the rights belonging to the Justiza, that a very small portion of power remained in the hands of the King. The Aragonese seem to have been sollicitous that their Monarchs should know and feel this state of impotence, to which they were reduced. Even in swearing allegiance to their sovereign, an act which ought, naturally, to be accompanied with professions of submission and respect, they devised an oath, in such a form, as to remind him of his dependance on his subjects. "We," said the Justiza to the King in the name of his high-spirited barons, "who are each of us as good, and who are altogether more powerful than you, promise obedience to your government, if you maintain our rights and liberties; but if not, not." Conformably to this oath, they established it as a fundamental article in their constitution, that if the King should violate their rights and privileges, it was lawful for the people to disclaim him as their sovereign, and to elect another in his place.[25] The attachment of the Aragonese to this singular constitution of government, was extreme, and their respect for it approached to superstitious veneration. In the preamble to one of their laws, they declare that such was the barrenness of their country, and the poverty of the inhabitants, that if it were not on account of the liberties by which they were distinguished from other nations, the people would abandon it, and go in quest of a settlement to some more fruitful region.[26]

In Castile, there were not such peculiarities in the form of government, as to establish any remarkable distinction between it, and that of the other European nations. The executive part of government was committed to the King, but with a prerogative extremely limited. The legislative authority resided in the Cortes, which was composed of the nobility, the dignified ecclesiasticks, and the representatives of the cities. The assembly of the Cortes in Castile was very ancient, and seems to have been coeval with the constitution. The members of the three different orders, who had a right of suffrage, met in one place, and deliberated as one collective body; the decisions of which were regulated by the sentiments of the majority. The right of imposing taxes, of enacting laws, and of redressing grievances belonged to this assembly; and in order to secure the assent of the King to such statutes and regulations, as were deemed salutary or beneficial to the kingdom, it was usual in the Cortes, to take no step towards granting money, until all business relative to the publick welfare was concluded. The representatives of cities seem to have obtained a seat very early in the Cortes of Castile, and soon acquired such influence and credit, as were very uncommon, at a period when the splendor and pre-eminence of the nobility had eclipsed or annihilated all other orders of men. The number of members from cities bore such a proportion to that of the whole collective body, as rendered them extremely respectable in the Cortes. The degree of consideration, which they possessed in the state, may be estimated by one event. Upon the death of John I, a council of regency was appointed to govern the kingdom during the minority of his son. It was composed of an equal number of noblemen, and of deputies chosen by the cities; the latter were admitted to the same rank, and invested with the same powers, as prelates and grandees of the first order.[27] But though the members of communities in Castile were elevated above the condition wherein they were placed in other kingdoms of Europe; though they had attained to such political importance, that even the proud and jealous spirit of the feudal aristocracy could not exclude them from some share of government; yet the nobles, notwithstanding these acquisitions of the commons, continued to assert the privileges of their order, in opposition to the crown, in a tone extremely high. There was not any body of nobility in Europe more distinguished for independance of spirit, haughtiness of deportment, and bold pretensions, than that of Castile. The history of that monarchy affords the most striking examples of the vigilance with which they observed, and of the vigour with which they opposed every scheme of their Kings, that tended to encroach on their jurisdiction, to diminish their dignity, or to abridge their power. Even in their ordinary intercourse with their Monarchs, they preserved such a consciousness of their rank, that the nobles of the first order claimed it as a privilege to be covered in the royal presence, and approached their sovereigns rather as equals than as subjects.

The constitution of the subordinate monarchies, which depended on the crowns of Castile and Aragon, nearly resembled that of the kingdom to which they were annexed. In all of them, the dignity and independance of the nobles were great; the immunities and power of the cities were considerable.

An attentive observation of the singular situation of Spain, as well as of the various events which occurred there, from the invasion of the Moors to the union of its kingdoms under Ferdinand and Isabella, will discover those causes, to which all the peculiarities in its political constitution, that I have pointed out, ought to be ascribed.

As the provinces of Spain were wrested from the Mahometans gradually and with difficulty, the nobles, who followed the standard of any eminent leader in these wars, conquered not for him alone, but for themselves. They claimed a share in the lands which their valour had torn from the enemy, and their prosperity and power increased, in proportion as the territory of the Prince extended.

During their perpetual wars with the Moors, the Monarchs of Spain depended so much on their nobles, that it became necessary to concilitate their good will by successive grants of new honours and privileges. By the time that any Prince could establish his dominion in a conquered province, the greater part of the property was parcelled out by him among his barons, with such jurisdiction and immunities as raised them almost to sovereign power.

At the same time, the kingdoms erected in so many different corners of Spain were extremely inconsiderable. The petty Monarch was but little elevated above his nobles. They, feeling themselves to be almost his equals, acted as such. The Kings of such limited domains could neither command much respect, nor possess great power; and noblemen, so nearly on the same level, could not look up to them with that reverence, with which the sovereigns of the great monarchies in Europe were viewed by their subjects.

These circumstances concurred in exalting the nobility, and in depressing the royal authority; there were others, which raised the cities in Spain to consideration and power.

As the open country, during the wars with the Moors, was perpetually exposed to the excursions of the enemy, with whom no peace or truce was so permanent as to prove any lasting security, self-preservation obliged persons of all ranks to fix their residence in places of strength. The castles of the barons, which, in other countries, afforded a commodious retreat from the depredations of banditti, or from the transient violence of any interior commotion, were unable to resist an enemy whose operations were conducted with regular and persevering vigour. Cities, in which great numbers united for their mutual defence, were the only places to which people could retire with any prospect of safety. To this was owing the rapid growth of those cities in Spain of which the Christians recovered possession. All who fled from the Moorish yoke resorted to them, as to an asylum; and there, the greater part of those, who took the field against the Mahometans, established their families.

Each of these cities, during a longer or shorter course of years, was the capital of a little state, and enjoyed all the advantages, which accelerate the increase of inhabitants in every place that is the seat of government.

The number of cities in Spain, at the beginning of the fifteenth century, was considerable, and they were peopled far
beyond the proportion which was common in other parts of
Europe, except in Italy and the Low-Countries. The Moors
had introduced manufactures into these cities, while under their
dominion. The Christians, who, by intermixture with them,
had learned their arts, continued to cultivate these. The trade
of several of the Spanish towns appears to have been considerable; and the spirit of commerce continued to preserve
the number of their inhabitants, as the sense of danger had first
induced them to crowd together.

As the Spanish cities were populous, many of the inhabitants were of a rank superior to those who resided in towns in
other countries of Europe. That cause, which contributed chiefly
to their population, affected equally persons of every condition,
who flocked thither promiscuously, in order to find shelter, or
in hopes of making a stand there against the enemy, with greater
advantage than in any other station. The persons elected as their
representatives in the Cortes by the cities, or promoted to offices
of trust and dignity in the government of the community, were
often, as will appear from transactions which I shall hereafter
relate, of such considerable rank in the kingdom, as reflected
lustre on their constituents, and on the stations wherein they
were placed.

As it was impossible to carry on a continual war against the
Moors, without some other military force, than that which
the barons were obliged to bring into the field, in consequence
of the feudal tenures, it became necessary to have some troops,
particularly a body of light cavalry, in constant pay. It was one
of the privileges of the nobles, that their lands were exempt
from the burden of taxes. The charge of supporting the troops
requisite for the publick safety, fell wholly upon the cities; and
their Kings, being obliged frequently to apply to them for aid,
found it necessary to gain their favour by concessions, which
extended their immunities, and added to their wealth and power.

When the influence of all these circumstances, peculiar to
Spain, is added to the general and common causes, which contrib-

uted to aggrandize cities in other countries of Europe, this will fully account for the extensive privileges which they acquired, as well as the extraordinary consideration to which they attained, in all the Spanish kingdoms.

By these exorbitant privileges of the nobility, and this unusual power of the cities in Spain, the royal prerogative was hemmed in on every hand, and reduced within very narrow bounds. Sensible of this, and impatient of such restraint, different Monarchs endeavoured, at various junctures, to enlarge their own jurisdiction, and to circumscribe that of their subjects. Their power, however, or their abilities were so unequal to the undertaking, that their efforts were attended with little success. But when Ferdinand and Isabella found themselves at the head of all the united kingdoms of Spain, and delivered from the danger and interruption of domestick wars, they were not only in a condition to resume, but were able to prosecute with advantage, the schemes of extending the prerogative, which their ancestors had attempted in vain. Ferdinand's profound sagacity in concerting his measures, his persevering industry in conducting them, and his uncommon address in carrying them into execution, fitted him admirably for an undertaking which required all these talents.

As the overgrown power, and high pretensions of the nobility were what the Monarchs of Spain felt most sensibly, and bore with the greatest impatience, the great object of Ferdinand's policy was to reduce these within more moderate bounds. Under various pretexts, sometimes by violence, more frequently in consequence of decrees obtained in the courts of law, he wrested from the barons a great part of the lands, which had been granted to them by the inconsiderate bounty of former Monarchs, particularly during the feeble and profuse reign of his predecessor Henry IV. He did not give the entire conduct of affairs to persons of noble birth, who were accustomed to occupy every department of importance in peace or in war, as if it had been a privilege peculiar to their order, to be employed as the sole counsellors and ministers of the crown. He often transacted business of great consequence without their intervention, and committed many offices of power and trust to new men, devoted to his interest.[28] He introduced a degree of state dignity into his court, which being unknown in Spain, while it remained split into many small kingdoms, taught the nobles to approach their sovereign with more ceremony, and gradually rendered him the object of greater deference and respect.

The annexing the masterships of the three military orders of St. Jago, Calatrava, and Alcantara, to the crown, was another expedient, by which Ferdinand greatly augmented the revenue and power of the Kings of Spain. These orders were instituted in imitation of those of the Knights Templars and of St. John of Jerusalem, on purpose to wage perpetual war with the Mahometans, and to protect the pilgrims who visited Compostella, or other places of eminent sanctity in Spain. The zeal and superstition of the ages, in which they were founded, prompted persons of every rank to bestow such liberal donations on these holy warriors, that, in a short time, they engrossed a considerable share in the property and wealth of the kingdom. The masterships of these orders came to be stations of the greatest power and opulence to which a Spanish nobleman could be advanced. These high dignities were in the disposal of the Knights of the Order, and placed the persons on whom they conferred them almost on a level with their sovereign. Ferdinand, unwilling that the nobility, whom he considered as already too formidable, should derive such additional credit and influence from possessing the government of these wealthy fraternities, was solicitous to wrest it out of their hands, and to vest it in the crown. His measures for accomplishing this, were wisely planned, and executed with vigour.[29] By address, by promises, and by threats, he prevailed on the Knights of each Order to place Isabella and him at the head of it. Innocent VIII and Alexander VI gave this election the sanction of papal authority;[30] and subsequent Pontiffs rendered the annexation of these masterships to the crown perpetual.

While Ferdinand, by this measure, diminished the power and influence of the nobility, and added new lustre or authority to the crown, he was taking other important steps with a view to the same object. The sovereign jurisdiction which the feudal barons exercised within their own territories, was the pride and distinction of their order. To have invaded openly a privilege which they prized so highly, and in defence of which they would have run so eagerly to arms, was a measure too daring for a Prince of Ferdinand's cautious temper. He took advantage, however, of an opportunity which the state of his kingdoms and the spirit of his people presented him, in order to undermine what he durst not assault. The incessant depredations of the Moors, the want of discipline among the troops which were employed to oppose them, the frequent civil wars between the crown and the nobility, as well as the undiscerning rage with which the barons carried on their private wars with each other, filled all the provinces of Spain with disorder. Rapine, outrage, and murder, became so common, as not only to interrupt commerce, but in a great measure to suspend all intercourse between one place and another. That security and protection which men expect from entering into civil society, ceased almost totally. Interior order and police, while the feudal institutions remained in vigour, were so little objects of attention, and the administration of justice was so extremely feeble, that it would have been vain to have expected relief from the established laws or the ordinary judges. But the evil became so intolerable, and the inhabitants of cities, who were the chief sufferers, grew so impatient of this anarchy, that self-preservation forced them to have recourse to an extraordinary remedy. About the middle of the thirteenth century, the cities in the kingdom of Aragon, and after their example those in Castile, formed themselves into an association, distinguished by the name of the *Holy Brotherhood*. They exacted a certain contribution from each of the associated towns; they levied a considerable body of troops, in order to protect travellers, and to pursue criminals; they appointed judges, who opened their courts in various parts of the kingdom. Whoever was guilty of murder, robbery, or of any act that violated the publick peace, and was seized by the troops of the *Brotherhood,* was carried before their own judges, who, without paying any regard to the exclusive and sovereign jurisdiction which the lord of the place might claim, tried and condemned the criminals. By means of this, the prompt and impartial administration of justice was restored; and together with it, internal tranquillity and order began to return. The nobles alone murmured at this salutary institution. They complained of it as an encroachment on one of their most valuable privileges. They remonstrated against it in an high tone; and, on some occasions, refused to grant any aid to the crown, unless it were abolished. Ferdinand, however, was sensible not only of the good effects of the Holy Brotherhood with respect to the police of his kingdoms, but perceived its tendency to abridge, and at length to annihilate the territorial jurisdiction of the nobility. He countenanced the institution on every occasion. He supported it with the whole force of royal authority; and besides the expedients employed by him in common with the other monarchs of Europe, he availed himself of this institution, which was peculiar to his kingdom, in order to limit and abolish that independant jurisdiction of the nobility, which was no less inconsistent with the authority of the Prince, than with the order of society.

But though Ferdinand by these measures considerably enlarged the boundaries of prerogative, and acquired a degree of influence and power far beyond what any of his predecessors had enjoyed, yet the limitations of the royal authority, and the barriers against its encroachments, continued to be many and strong. The spirit of liberty was vigorous among the people of Spain; the spirit of independance was high among the nobility; and though the love of glory, peculiar to the Spaniards in every period of their history, prompted them to support Ferdinand with zeal in his foreign operations, and to afford him such aid as enabled him not only to undertake but to execute great enterprizes; he reigned over his subjects with a jurisdiction less extensive than that of any of the great monarchs in Europe. It will appear from many passages in the following history, that, during a considerable part of the reign of his successor Charles V the prerogative of the Spanish crown was equally circumscribed.

The ancient government and laws in France so nearly resembled those of the other feudal kingdoms, that such a detail with respect to them as was necessary, in order to convey some idea of the nature and effects of the peculiar institutions which took place in Spain, would be superfluous. In the view which I have exhibited of the means by which the French monarchs acquired such full command of the national force of their kingdom, as enabled them to engage in extensive schemes of foreign operation, I have already pointed out the great steps by which they advanced towards a more ample possession of political power, and a more uncontrouled exercise of their royal prerogative. All that now remains is to take notice of such particulars in the constitution of France, as serve either to distinguish it from that of other countries, or tend to throw any light on the transactions of that period to which the following history extends.

Under the French monarchs of the first race, the royal prerogative was very inconsiderable. The General Assemblies of the nation, which met annually at stated seasons, extended their authority to every department of government. The power of electing Kings, of enacting laws, of redressing grievances, of passing judgment in the last resort, with respect to every person and to every cause, and of conferring donations on the Prince, resided in this great convention of the nation. Under the second race of Kings, notwithstanding the power and splendour which the conquests of Charlemagne added to the crown, the general assemblies of the nations continued to possess extensive authority. The right of determining which of the royal family should be placed on the throne was vested in them. The monarchs elected by their suffrage were accustomed regularly to call and to consult them with respect to every affair of importance to the state, and without their consent no law was passed, and no new tax was levied.

But, by the time that Hugh Capet, the father of the third race of Kings, took possession of the throne of France, such changes had happened in the political state of the kingdom, as considerably affected the power and jurisdiction of the general assembly of the nation. The royal authority in the hands of the degenerate posterity of Charlemagne, had dwindled into insignificance and contempt. Every considerable proprietor of land had formed his territory into a barony, almost independant of the sovereign. The dukes or governors of provinces, the counts or governors of towns and small districts, and the great officers of the crown, had rendered these dignities, originally granted only during pleasure or for life, hereditary in their families. Each of these had usurped all the rights which hitherto had been deemed the distinctions of royalty, particularly the privileges of dispensing justice within their own domains, of coining money, and of waging war. Every district was governed by local customs, acknowledged a distinct lord, and pursued a separate interest. The formality of doing homage to their sovereign, was almost the only act of subjection which haughty barons would perform, and that bound them no farther than they were willing to acknowledge its obligation.

In a kingdom broken into so many independant baronies, hardly any common principle of union remained; and the general assembly in its deliberations could scarce consider the nation as forming one body, or establish common regulations to be of equal force in every part. Within the immediate domains of the crown the King might publish laws, and they were obeyed, because there he was acknowledged as the only lord. But if he had aimed at rendering these general, that would have alarmed the barons as an encroachment upon the independance of their jurisdiction. The barons, with no less care, avoided the enacting of general laws, because the execution of them must have been vested in the King, and would have enlarged that paramount power which was the object of their jealousy. Thus, under the descendants of Hugh Capet, the States General (for that was the name by which the supreme assembly of the French nation came then to be distinguished) lost their legislative authority, or at least entirely relinquished the exercise of it. From that period, the jurisdiction of the States General extended no farther than to the imposition of new taxes, the determination of questions with respect to the right of succession to the crown, the settling of the regency when the preceding monarch had not fixed it by his will, and the presenting remonstrances enumerating the grievances of which the nation wished to obtain redress.

As, during several centuries, the monarchs of Europe seldom demanded extraordinary subsidies of their subjects, and the other events which required the interposition of the States, rarely occurred, their meetings in France were not frequent. They were summoned occasionally by their Kings, when compelled by their wants or by their fears have recourse to their aid; but they did not, like the Diet in Germany, the Cortes in Spain, or the Parliament in England, form an essential member of the constitution, the regular exertion of whose powers was requisite to give vigour and order to government.

When the States of France ceased to exercise legislative authority, the Kings began to assume it. They ventured at first on acts of legislation with great reserve; and after taking every precaution that could prevent their subjects from being alarmed at the exercise of a new power. They did not at once issue their ordinances in a tone of authority and command. They treated with their subjects; they pointed out what was best; and allured them to comply with it. By degrees, however, as the prerogative of the crown extended, and as the supreme jurisdiction of the royal courts came to be established, the Kings of France assumed more openly the stile and authority of law-givers, and before the beginning of the fifteenth century, the complete legislative power was vested in them.

Having secured this important acquisition, the steps that led to the right of imposing taxes were rendered few and easy. The people, accustomed to see their sovereigns, by their sole authority, issue ordinances which regulated points of the greatest consequence with respect to the property of their subjects, were not alarmed when they were required, by the royal edicts, to contribute certain sums towards supplying the exigencies of government, and carrying forward the measures of the nation. When Charles VII and Louis XI first ventured to exercise this new power, in the manner which I have already described, the gradual increase of the royal authority had so imperceptibly prepared the minds of the people of France for this innovation, that it excited no commotion in the kingdom, and seems scarce to have given rise to any murmur or complaint.

When the Kings of France had thus engrossed every power which can be exerted in government; when the right of making laws, of levying money, of keeping an army of mercenaries in constant pay, of declaring war and of concluding peace centered in the crown, the constitution of the kingdom, which, under the first race of Kings, was nearly democratical, which, under the second race, became an aristocracy, terminated, under the third race, in a pure monarchy. Every thing that tended to preserve the appearance, or revive the memory of the ancient mixed government, seems from that period to have been industriously avoided. During the long and active reign of Francis I the variety as well as extent of whose operations obliged him to lay many heavy impositions on his subjects, the States General of France were not once assembled, nor were the people once allowed to exert the power of taxing themselves, which, according to the original ideas of feudal government, was a right essential to every free-man.

Two things, however, remained, which moderated the exercise of the regal prerogative, and restrained it within such bounds as preserved the constitution of France from degenerating into mere despotism. The rights and privileges claimed by the nobility must be considered as one barrier against the absolute dominion of the crown. Though the nobles of France had lost that political power which was vested in their order as a body, they still retained the personal rights and pre-eminence which they derived from their rank. They preserved a consciousness of elevation above other classes of citizens; an exemption from burdens to which they were subject; a contempt of the occupations in which they were engaged; the privilege of assuming ensigns that indicated their dignity; a title to be treated with a certain degree of deference during peace; and a claim to various distinctions when in the field. Many of these pretensions were not founded on the words of statutes, or derived from positive laws; they were defined and ascertained by the maxims of honour, a title more delicate, but no less sacred. These rights, established and protected by a principle equally vigilant in guarding, and intrepid in defending them, are to the Sovereign himself objects of respect and veneration. Wherever they stand in its way, the royal prerogative is bounded. The violence of a Despot may exterminate such an order of men; but as long as it subsists, and its ideas of personal distinction remain entire, the power of the Prince has limits.[31]

As in France, the body of nobility was very numerous, and retained an high sense of their own pre-eminence, to this we may ascribe, in a great measure, the mode of exercising the royal prerogative which peculiarly distinguishes the government of that kingdom. An intermediate order was placed between the Monarch and his other subjects, and in every act of authority it became necessary to attend to its privileges, and not only to guard against any real violation of these, but to avoid any suspicion of its being possible that they might be violated. Thus a species of government was established in France, unknown in the ancient world, that of a monarchy, in which the power of the sovereign, though unconfined by any legal or constitutional restraint, has certain bounds set to it by the ideas which one class of his subjects entertain concerning their own dignity.

The jurisdiction of the Parliaments of France, particularly that of Paris, was the other barrier which served to confine the exercise of the royal prerogative within certain limits. The parliament of Paris was originally the court of the Kings of France, to which they committed the supreme administration of justice within their own domains, as well as the power of deciding with respect to all cases brought before it by appeals from the courts of the barons. When the time and place of its meeting were fixed, when not only the form of its procedure, but the principles on which it decided, were rendered regular and consistent, when every cause of importance was finally determined there, and when the people became accustomed to resort thither as to the supreme temple of justice, the parliament of Paris rose to high estimation in the kingdom, its members acquired dignity, and its decrees were submitted to, with deference. The Kings of France, when they first began to assume the legislative power, in order to reconcile the minds of their people to this new exertion of prerogative, produced their edicts and ordinances in the parliament of Paris, that they might be approved of and registered there, before they were published and declared to be of authority in the kingdom. During the intervals between the meetings of the States General of the kingdom, or under those reigns when the States General were not assembled, the Monarchs of France were accustomed to consult the parliament of Paris with respect to the most arduous affairs of government, and frequently regulated their conduct by its advice, in declaring war, in concluding peace, and in other transactions of publick concern. Thus there was erected in the kingdom a tribunal which became the great depository of the laws, and by the uniform tenor of its decrees it established principles of justice and forms of proceeding which were considered as so sacred, that even the sovereign power of the Monarch durst not venture to disregard or to violate them. The members of this illustrious body, though they neither possess legislative authority, nor can be considered as the representatives of the people, have availed themselves of the reputation and influence which they had acquired among their countrymen, in order to make a stand to the utmost of their ability against every unprecedented and exorbitant exertion of the prerogative. In every period of the French history, they have merited the praise of being the virtuous but feeble guardians of the rights and privileges of the nation.

The kingdom extends to the confines of the German Empire, from which Charles V derived his title of highest dignity. In explaining the political constitution of this vast and complex body at the beginning of the sixteenth century, I shall avoid entering into such a detail as would involve my readers in that inextricable labyrinth, which it formed by the multiplicity of its tribunals, the number of its members, their interfering rights, and by the endless discussions or refinements of the publick lawyers of Germany with respect to all these.

The Empire of Charlemagne was a structure erected in so short a time that it could not be permanent. Under his immediate successor it began to totter; and it soon fell to pieces. The crown of Germany was separated for ever from that of France, and the descendants of Charlemagne established two great monarchies so situated as to give rise to a perpetual rivalship and enmity between them. But the Princes of the race of Charlemagne who were placed on the Imperial throne, were not altogether so degenerate, as those of the same family who reigned in France. In the hands of the former the royal authority retained some vigour, and the nobles of Germany, though possessed of extensive privileges as well as ample territories, did not so early attain independance. The great offices of the crown continued to be at the disposal of the sovereign, and during a long period, fiefs remained in their original state, without becoming hereditary and perpetual in the families to which they had been granted.

At length the German branch of the family of Charlemagne became extinct, and his feeble descendants who reigned in France had sunk into such contempt, that the Germans, without looking towards them, exercised the right inherent in a free people; and in a general assembly of the nation elected Conrad Count of Franconia Emperor. After him Henry of Saxony, and his descendants the three Othos, were placed, in succession, on the Imperial throne, by the suffrages of their countrymen. The extensive territories of the Saxon Emperors, their eminent abilities and enterprizing genius not only added new vigour to the Imperial dignity, but raised it to higher power and pre-eminence. Otho the Great marched at the head of a numerous army into Italy, and after the example of Charlemagne, gave law to that country. Every power there recognized his authority. He created Popes and deposed them by his sovereign mandate. He annexed the kingdom of Italy to the German Empire. Elated with his success, he assumed the title of Cæsar Augustus;[32] and a Prince born in the heart of Germany pretended to be the successor of the Emperors of ancient Rome, and claimed a right to the same power and prerogative.

But while the Emperors, by means of these new titles, and new dominions, gradually acquired additional power and splendour, the nobility of Germany went on at the same time extending their privileges and jurisdiction. The situation of affairs was favourable to their attempts. The vigour which Charlemagne had given to government quickly relaxed. The inability of some of his successors was such, as would have encouraged vassals less enterprizing than the nobles of that age, to have claimed new rights and to have assumed new powers. The civil wars in which other Emperors were engaged, obliged them to pay perpetual court to their subjects on whose support they depended, and not only to connive at their usurpations, but to permit and even to authorize them. Fiefs became gradually hereditary. They were transmitted not only in the direct, but in the collateral line. The investiture of them was demanded not only by male but by female heirs. Every baron began to exercise sovereign jurisdiction within his own domains; and the Dukes and Counts of Germany took wide steps towards rendering their territories distinct and independent States.[33] The Saxon Emperors observed their progress, and were aware of its tendency. But as they could not hope to humble vassals already grown too potent, unless they had turned their whole force as well as attention to that enterprize, and as they were extremely intent on their expeditions into Italy, which they could not undertake without the concurrence of their nobles, they were sollicitous not to alarm them by any direct attack on their privileges and jurisdictions. They aimed, however, at undermining their power, and inconsiderately bestowed additional territories, and accumulated new honours on the clergy, in hopes that this order might serve as a counterpoise to that of the nobility in any future struggle.[34]

The unhappy effects of this fatal error in policy were quickly felt. Under the Emperors of the Franconian and Swabian lines, whom the Germans by their voluntary election placed on the Imperial throne, a new face of things appeared, and a scene was exhibited in Germany, which astonished all Christendom at that time, and which in the present age appears almost incredible. The Popes, hitherto dependant on the Emperors, and indebted for their power as well as dignity to their beneficence and protection, began to claim a superior jurisdiction; and in virtue of authority which they pretended to derive from heaven, tried, condemned, excommunicated and deposed their former masters. Nor is this to be considered merely as a frantick sally of passion

135

in a pontiff intoxicated with high ideas concerning the extent of priestly domination, and the plentitude of papal power. Gregory VII was able as well as daring. His presumption and violence were accompanied with political discernment and sagacity. He had observed that the Princes and nobles of Germany, had acquired such considerable territories and such extensive jurisdiction as rendered them not only formidable to the Emperors, but disposed them to favour any attempt to circumscribe their power. He foresaw that the ecclesiasticks of Germany, raised almost to a level with its Princes, were ready to support any person who would stand forth as the protector of their privileges and independance. With both of these Gregory negociated, and had secured many devoted adherents among them, before he ventured to enter the lists against the head of the Empire.

He began his rupture with Henry IV upon a pretext that was popular and plausible. He complained of the venality and corruption with which the Emperor had granted the investiture of benefices to ecclesiasticks. He contended that this right belonged to him as head of the church; he required Henry to confine himself within the bounds of his civil jurisdiction, and to abstain for the future from such sacrilegious encroachment on his spiritual dominion. All the censures of the church were denounced against Henry, because he refused to relinquish those powers which his predecessors had uniformly exercised. The most considerable of the German Princes and ecclesiasticks were excited to take arms against him. His mother, his wife, his sons were wrought upon to disregard all the ties of blood as well as of duty, and to join the party of his enemies.[35] Such were the successful arts with which the court of Rome inflamed the superstitious zeal and conducted the factious spirit of the Germans and Italians, that an Emperor, distinguished not only for many virtues, but possessed of considerable talents, was at length obliged to appear as a supplicant at the gate of the castle in which the Pope resided, and to stand there, three days, barefooted, in the depth of winter, imploring a pardon, which at length he obtained with difficulty.

This act of humiliation degraded the Imperial dignity. Nor was the depression only momentary. The contest between Gregory and Henry give rise to the two great factions of the Guelfs and Ghibellines; the former of which supporting the pretensions of the Popes, and the latter defending the rights of the Emperor, kept Germany and Italy in perpetual agitation during three centuries. A regular system for humbling the Emperors and circumscribing their power was formed, and adhered to uniformly throughout that period. The Popes, the free States in Italy, the nobility and ecclesiasticks of Germany, were all interested in its success; and notwithstanding the return of some short intervals of vigour, under the administration of a few able Emperors, the Imperial authority continued to decline. During the anarchy of the long interregnum subsequent to the death of William of Holland, it dwindled down to nothing. Rodulph of Hapsburgh, the founder of the house of Austria, and who first opened the way to its future grandeur, was at length elected Emperor, not that he might re-establish and extend the Imperial authority, but because his territories and influence were so inconsiderable as not to excite the jealousy of the German Princes, who were willing to preserve the forms of a constitution, the power and vigour of which they had destroyed. Several of his successors were placed on the Imperial throne from the same motive; and almost every remaining prerogative was wrested out of the hands of feeble Princes unable to exercise or defend them.

During this period of turbulence and confusion the constitution of the Germanick body underwent a total change. The ancient names of courts and magistrates, together with the original forms and appearance of policy were preserved; but such new privileges and jurisdictions were assumed, and so many various rights established, that the same species of government no longer subsisted. The Princes, the great nobility, the dignified ecclesiasticks, the free cities had taken advantage of the interregnum, which I have mentioned, to establish or to extend their usurpations. They claimed and exercised the right of governing their respective territories with full sovereignty. They acknowledged no superior with respect to any point, relative to the interior administration and police of their domains. They enacted laws, imposed taxes, coined money, declared war, concluded peace, and exerted every prerogative peculiar to independant States. The ideas of order and political union which had formed the various provinces of Germany into one body were entirely lost; and the society must have dissolved, if the forms of feudal subordination had not preserved such an appearance of connection or dependance among the various members of the community, as preserved it from falling to pieces.

This bond of union, however, was extremely feeble; and no principle remained in the German constitution of sufficient force to maintain publick order, and hardly to ascertain personal security. From the accession of Rodulph of Hapsburgh, to the reign of Maximilian, the immediate predecessor of Charles V the Empire felt every calamity which a state must endure when the authority of government is so much relaxed as to have lost all vigour. The causes of dissention among that vast number of members which composed the Germanick body, were infinite and unavoidable. These gave rise to perpetual private wars, carried on with all the violence of resentment when unrestrained by superior authority. Rapine, outrage, exactions, became universal. Commerce was interrupted; industry suspended; and every part of Germany resembled a country which an enemy had plundered and laid desolate. The variety of expedients employed with a view to restore order and tranquillity, prove that the grievances occasioned by this state of anarchy had grown intolerable. Arbiters were appointed to terminate the differences among the several states. The cities united in a league, the object of which was to check the rapine and extortions of the nobility. The nobility formed confederacies, on purpose to maintain tranquillity among their own order. Germany was divided into several Circles, in each of which a provincial and partial jurisdiction was established, to supply the place of a publick and common tribunal.[36]

But all these remedies were so fruitless, that they served only to demonstrate the violence of that anarchy which prevailed, and the inefficacy of the means employed to correct it. At length Maximilian, by instituting the Imperial chamber, a tribunal composed of judges named partly by the Emperor, partly by the several States, and vested with authority to decide finally concerning all differences among the members of the Germanick body, re-established publick order in the Empire. A few years after, by giving a new form to the Aulick council, which takes cognizance of all feudal causes, and such as belong to the Emperor's immediate jurisdiction, he restored some degree of vigour to the Imperial authority.

But notwithstanding the salutary effects of these regulations and improvements, the political constitution of the German Empire, at the commencement of the period of which I propose to write the history, was of a species so peculiar, as not to resemble perfectly any form of government known either in the ancient or modern world. It was a complex body, formed by the association of several States, each of which possessed sovereign and independant jurisdiction within its own territories. Of all the members which composed this united body, the Emperor was the head. In his name, all decrees and regulations with respect to points of common concern, were issued; and to him the power of carrying them into execution was committed. But this appearance of monarchical power in the Emperor was more than counterbalanced by the influence and authority of the Princes and States of the Empire in every act of administration. No law extending to the whole body could pass, no resolution that affected the general interest could be taken, without the approbation of the Diet of the Empire. In this assembly, every sovereign Prince and State of the Germanick body had a right to be present, to deliberate, and to vote. The decrees or *Recesses* of the Diet were the laws of the Empire, which the Emperor was bound to ratify and enforce.

Under this aspect the constitution of the Empire appears a regular confederacy, similar to the Achæan league in ancient Greece, or to that of the United Provinces and of the Swiss cantons in modern times. But if viewed in another light, striking peculiarities in its political state present themselves. The Germanick body was not formed by the union of members altogether distinct and independant. All the Princes and States joined in this association, were originally subject to the Emperors, and acknowledged them as sovereigns. Besides this, they originally held their lands as Imperial fiefs, and in consequence of this tenure owed the Emperors all those services which feudal vassals are bound to perform to their liege lord. But though this political subjection was entirely at an end, and the influence of the feudal relation much diminished, the ancient forms and institutions introduced when the Emperors governed Germany with authority, not inferior to that which the other monarchs of Europe possessed, still remained. Thus an opposition was established between the genius of the government, and the forms of administration in the German Empire. The former considered the Emperor only as the head of a confederacy, the members of which, by their voluntary choice, have raised him to that dignity; the latter seemed to imply, that he is really invested with sovereign power. By this circumstance, such principles of hostility and discord were interwoven in the frame of the Germanick body, as affected each of its members, rendering their interior union incomplete, and their external efforts feeble and irregular. The effects of this vice or disorder inherent in the constitution of the Empire are so considerable, that, without attending to them, it is impossible to comprehend many transactions in the reign of Charles V or to form just ideas concerning the genius of the German government.

The Emperors of Germany, at the beginning of the sixteenth century, were distinguished by the most pompous titles, and by such ensigns of dignity as intimated their authority to be superior to that of all other monarchs. The greatest Princes of the Empire attended and served them on some occasions, as the officers of their household. They exercised prerogatives which no other sovereign ever claimed. They retained pretensions to all the extensive powers which their predecessors had enjoyed in any former age. But at the same time, instead of possessing that ample domain which had belonged to the ancient Emperors of Germany, and which stretched from Basil to Cologne, along both banks of the Rhine,[37] they were stript of all territorial property, and had not a single city, a single castle, a single foot of land, that pertained to them as heads of the Empire. As their domain was alienated, their stated revenues were reduced almost to nothing; and the extraordinary aids which on a few occasions they obtained, were granted sparingly, and paid with reluctance. The Princes and States of the Empire, though they seemed to recognize the Imperial authority, were subjects only in name, each of them possessing a compleat municipal jurisdiction within the precincts of his own territories.

From this ill-compacted frame of government, effects that were unavoidable resulted. The Emperors, dazzled with the splendour of their titles, and the exterior signs of vast authority, were apt to imagine themselves to be the real sovereigns of Germany, and were led to aim continually at recovering the exercise of those powers and prerogatives which the forms of the constitution seemed to vest in them, and which their predecessors Charlemagne and the Otho's had actually enjoyed. The Princes and States, aware of the nature as well as extent of their pretensions, were perpetually on their guard, in order to watch all the motions of the Imperial court, and to circumscribe its power within limits still more narrow. The Emperors, in support of their claims, appealed to ancient forms and institutions, which the States held to be obsolete. The States founded their rights on recent practice and modern privileges, which the Emperors considered as usurpations.

This jealousy of the Imperial authority, together with the opposition between it and the rights of the States, increased considerably from the time that the Emperors were elected, not by the collective body of German nobles, but by a few Princes of chief dignity. During a long period, all the members of the Germanick body assembled, and made choice of the person whom they appointed to be their head. But amidst the violence and anarchy which prevailed for several centuries in the Empire, seven Princes who possessed the most extensive territories, and who had obtained a hereditary title to the great offices of the State, acquired the exclusive privilege of nominating the Emperor. This right was confirmed to them by the Golden Bull; the mode of exercising it was ascertained, and they were dignified with the appellation of *Electors*. The nobility and free-cities being thus stripped of a privilege which they had once enjoyed, were less connected with a Prince, towards whose elevation they had not contributed by their suffrages, and came to be more apprehensive of his authority. The Electors, by their extensive power, and the distinguishing privileges which they possessed, became formidable to the Emperors, with whom they were placed almost on a level in several acts of jurisdiction. Thus the introduction of the Electoral college into the Empire, and the authority which it acquired, instead of diminishing, contributed to strengthen the principles of hostility and discord in the Germanick constitution.

These were further augmented by the various and repugnant forms of civil policy in the several States which composed the Germanick body. It is no easy matter to render the union of independant States perfect and entire, even when the genius and forms of their respective governments happen to be altogether similar. But in the German Empire, which was a confederacy of Princes, of Ecclesiasticks, and of free-cities, it was impossible that they could incorporate thoroughly. The free-cities were small republicks, in which the maxims and spirit peculiar to that species of government prevailed. The Princes and nobles to whom supreme jurisdiction belonged, possessed a sort of monarchical power within their own territories, and the forms of their interior administration nearly resembled those of the great feudal kingdoms. The interests, the ideas, the objects of States so differently constituted, cannot be the same. Nor could their common deliberations be carried on with the same spirit, while the love of liberty and attention to commerce were the reigning principles in the cities; together with the desire of power and ardour for military glory, were the governing passions of the Princes and nobility.

The secular and ecclesiastical members of the Empire were as little fitted for union as the free-cities and the nobility. Vast territories were annexed to several of the German bishopricks and abbeys, and the dignified ecclesiasticks held some of the highest offices in the Empire by hereditary right. The younger sons of noblemen of the second order, who had devoted themselves to the church, were commonly promoted to these stations of eminence and power; and it was no small mortification to the Princes and great nobility to see persons raised from an inferior rank to the same level with themselves, or even exalted to superior dignity. The education of these churchmen, the genius of their profession, and their connection with the court of Rome, rendered their character as well as interest different from those of the other members of the Germanick body, with whom they were called to act in concert. Thus another source of jealousy and variance was opened, which ought not to be overlooked when we are searching into the nature of the German constitution.

To all these causes of dissention may be added one more, arising from the unequal distribution of power and wealth among the States of the Empire. The electors, and other nobles of the highest rank, not only possessed sovereign jurisdiction, but governed such extensive, populous, and rich countries, as rendered them great Princes. Many of the other members, though they enjoyed all the rights of sovereignty, ruled over such petty domains, that their real power bore no proportion to this high prerogative. A well-compacted and vigorous confederacy could not be formed of such dissimilar states. The weaker were jealous, timid, and unable either to assert or to defend their just privileges. The more powerful were apt to assume and to become oppressive. The Electors and Emperors endeavoured by turns to extend their own authority, by encroaching on the rights of these feeble members of the Germanick body; and they, over-awed or corrupted, tamely gave up their privileges, or meanly favoured the designs formed against them.

After contemplating all these principles of disunion and opposition in the constitution of the German Empire, it will be easy to account for the want of concord and uniformity, conspicuous in its councils and proceedings. That slow, dilatory, distrustful and irresolute spirit, which characterizes all its deliberations, will appear natural in a body, the junction of whose members was so incompleat, the different parts of which were held together by such feeble ties, and set at variance by such powerful motives. But the Empire of Germany, nevertheless, comprehended countries of such vast extent, and was inhabited by such a martial and hardy race of men, that when the abilities of an Emperor, or zeal for any common cause, could rouze this unwieldy body to put forth its strength, it acted with irresistible force. In the following history we shall find, that as the measures on which Charles V was most intent, were often thwarted or rendered abortive by the spirit of jealousy and division peculiar to the Germanick constitution; so it was by the influence which he acquired over the Princes of the Empire, and by engaging them to co-operate with him, that he was enabled to make some of the greatest efforts which distinguish his reign.

The Turkish history is so blended, during the reign of Charles V with that of the great nations in Europe, and the Ottoman Porte interposed so often, and with such decisive influence, in the wars and negociations of the Christian Princes, that some previous account of the state of government in that great Empire, is no less necessary for the information of my readers, than these views of the constitution of other kingdoms which I have already exhibited to them.

It has been the fate of the more southern and fertile parts of Asia, at different periods, to be conquered by that warlike and hardy race of men, who inhabit the vast country known to the ancients by the name of Scythia, and among the moderns by that of Tartary. One tribe of these people, called Turks or Turcomans, extended its conquests, under various leaders, and during several centuries, from the shore of the Caspian to the straits of the Dardanelles. Towards the middle of the fifteenth century, these formidable conquerors took Constantinople by storm, and established the seat of their government in that Imperial city. Greece, Moldavia, Walachia, and the other provinces of the ancient kingdoms of Thrace and Macedonia, together with part of Hungary, were subjected to their power.

But though the seat of the Turkish government was fixed in Europe, and the Sultans obtained possession of such extensive dominions in that quarter of the globe, the genius of their policy was purely Asiatick; and may be properly termed a despotism, in contradiction to these monarchical and republican forms of government which we have been hitherto contemplating. The supreme power was vested in Sultans of the Ottoman race, that blood being deemed so sacred, that no other was thought worthy of the throne. From this elevation, these sovereigns could look down, and behold all their subjects reduced to the same level before them. The maxims of Turkish policy admit not any of those institutions, which, in other countries, limit the exercise, or moderate the rigour of monarchical power. No great court with constitutional and permanent jurisdiction to interpose both in the enactment and execution of laws. No body of hereditary nobles, whose sense of their own pre-eminence, whose consciousness of what is due to their rank and character, whose jealousy of their privileges circumscribe the authority of the Prince, and serve not only as a barrier against the excesses of his caprice, but stand as an intermediate order between him and the people. Under the Turkish government, the political condition of every subject is equal. To be employed in the service of the Sultan, is the only circumstance that confers distinction. Even this distinction is annexed so closely to the stations in which persons serve, that it is scarce communicated to those who are placed in them. The highest dignity in the Empire does not give any rank or pre-eminence to the family of him who enjoys it. As every man, before he is raised to any station of authority, must go through the preparatory discipline of a long and servile obedience,[38] the moment he is deprived of power, he and his posterity return to the same condition with other subjects, and sink back into obscurity. It is the distinguishing and odious characteristic of the Eastern despotism, that it annihilates all other ranks of men, in order to exalt the monarch; that it leaves nothing to the former, while it gives every thing to the latter; that it endeavours to fix in the minds of those who are subject to it, the idea of no relation between men, but that of a master and of a slave, the former destined to command and punish, the latter formed to tremble and to obey.

But as there are circumstances which frequently obstruct or defeat the salutary effects of the best-regulated governments, there are others which contribute to mitigate the evils of the most vicious forms of policy. There can, indeed, be no constitutional restraints on the will of a Prince in a despotic government; but there may be such as are accidental. Absolute as the Turkish Sultans are, they feel themselves circumscribed both by religion, the principle on which their authority is founded,[39] and by the army, the instrument which they must employ in order to maintain it. Wherever religion interposes, the will of the Sovereign must submit to its decrees. When the Koran hath prescribed any religious rite; hath enjoined any moral duty; or hath confirmed, by its sanction, any political maxim, the command of the Sultan cannot overturn that which an higher authority hath established. The chief restriction, however, on the will of the Sultans, is imposed by the military power. An armed force must surround the throne of every Despot, to maintain his authority, and to execute his commands. As the Turks extended their empire over nations, which they did not exterminate, but reduce to subjection, they found it necessary to render their military establishment numerous and formidable. Amurath, their third Sultan, in order to form a body of devoted troops, that might serve as the immediate guards of his person and dignity, appointed his officers to seize annually, as the Imperial property, the fifth part of the youth taken in war. These, after being instructed in the Mahometan religion, inured to obedience by severe discipline, and trained to warlike exercises, were formed into a body distinguished by the name of *Janizaries*, or new soldiers. Every sentiment which enthusiasm can inspire, every mark of distinction that the favour of the Prince could confer, were employed in order to animate this body with martial ardour, and with a consciousness of its own pre-eminence.[40] The Janizaries soon became the chief strength and pride of the Ottoman armies; and by their number as well as reputation, were distinguished above all the troops, whose duty it was to attend on the person of the Sultans.

Thus, as the supreme power in every society is possessed by those who have arms in their hands, this formidable body of soldiers, destined to be the instruments of enlarging the Sultan's authority, acquired, at the same time, the means of controuling it. The Janizaries in Constantinople, like the Prætorian bands in ancient Rome, quickly perceived all the advantages which they derived from being stationed in the capital; from their union under one standard; and from being masters of the person of the Prince. The Sultans became no less sensible of their influence and importance. The *Capiculy*, or soldiery of the Porte, was the only power in the Empire that a Sultan or his Visier had reason to dread. To preserve the fidelity and attachment of the Janizaries, was the great art of government, and the principal object of attention in the policy of the Ottoman court. Under a monarch, whose abilities and vigour of mind fit him for command, they are obsequious instruments; execute whatever he enjoins; and render his power irresistible. Under feeble Princes, or such as are unfortunate, they become turbulent and mutinous; assume the tone of masters; degrade and exalt Sultans at pleasure; and teach those to tremble, on whose nod, at other times, life or death depend.

From Mahomet II who took Constantinople, to Solyman, who began his reign a few months after Charles V was placed on the Imperial throne, a succession of illustrious Princes ruled over the Turkish Empire. By their great abilities, they kept their subjects of every order, military as well as civil, submissive to government; and had the absolute command of whatever force their vast Empire was able to exert. Solyman, in particular, who is known to the Christians chiefly as a conqueror, but is celebrated in the Turkish annals as the great law-giver who established order and police in their Empire, governed during his long reign with no less authority than wisdom. He divided his dominions into several districts; he appointed the number of soldiers which each should furnish; he appropriated a certain proportion of the lands in every province for their maintenance; he regulated, with a minute accuracy, every thing relative to their discipline, their arms, and the nature of their service. He put the finances of the Empire into an orderly train of administration; and though the taxes in the Turkish dominions, as well as in the other despotic monarchies of the East, are far from being considerable, he supplied that defect by an attentive and severe œconomy.

Nor was it only under such Sultans as Solyman, whose talents were no less adapted to preserve interior order, than to conduct the operations of war, that the Turkish Empire engaged with advantage in its contests with the Christian states. The long succession of able Princes, which I have mentioned, had given such vigour and firmness to the Ottoman government, that it seems to have attained, during the sixteenth century, the highest degree of perfection of which its constitution was capable. Whereas the great monarchies in Christendom were still far from that state, which could enable them to act with a full exertion of their force. Besides this, the Turkish troops in that age possessed every advantage which arises from superiority in military discipline. At the time when Solyman began his reign, the Janizaries had been embodied near a century and a half, and during that long period the severity of their military discipline had in no degree relaxed. The soldiers drawn from the provinces of the Empire had been kept almost continually under arms, in the various wars which the Sultans had carried on with hardly any interval of peace. Against troops thus trained and accustomed to service, the forces of the Christian powers took the field with great disadvantage. The most intelligent as well as impartial authors of the sixteenth century, acknowledge and lament the superior attainments of the Turks in the military art. The success which uniformly attended their arms in all their wars, demonstrates the justness of this observation. The Christian armies did not acquire that superiority over the Turks, which they now possess, until the long establishment of standing forces had improved military discipline among the former; and until various causes and events, which it is not my province to explain, had corrupted or abolished their ancient warlike institutions among the latter.

Proofs and Illustrations

Only 3 of the 44 Proofs and Illustrations which follow the "View on the Progress of Society in Europe" are reproduced here.

[Note to p. 15: On the Institutions and Customs of the Barbarian Invaders of the Roman Empire]

I HAVE observed . . . that our only certain information concerning the ancient state of the barbarous nations must be derived from the Greek and Roman writers. Happily an account of the institutions and customs of one people, to which those of all the rest seem to have been in a great measure similar, has been transmitted to us by two authors, the most capable, perhaps, that ever wrote, of observing them with profound discernment, and of describing them with propriety and force. The reader must perceive that I have Cæsar and Tacitus in my eye. The former gives a short account of the ancient Germans in a few chapters of the sixth book of his commentaries: The latter wrote a treatise expressly on that subject. These are the most precious and instructive monuments of antiquity to the present inhabitants of Europe. From them we learn, (1.) That the state of Society among the ancient Germans was of the rudest and most simple form. They subsisted entirely by hunting or pasturage. Cæs. lib. vi. c. 21. They neglected agriculture, and lived chiefly on milk, cheese, and flesh. Ibid. c. 22. Tacitus agrees with him in most of these points; de morib. Germ. c. 14, 15, 23. The Goths were equally negligent of agriculture. Prisc. Rhet. ap. Byz. Script. v. i. p. 31. B. Society was in the same state among the Huns, who disdained to cultivate the earth, or to touch a plough. Amm. Marcel. lib. xxxi. p. 475. The same manners took place among the Alans; ibid. p. 477. While society remains in this simple state, men by uniting together scarce relinquish any portion of their natural independance. Accordingly we are informed, (2) That the authority of civil government was extremely limited among the Germans. During times of peace they had no common or fixed magistrate, but the chief men of every district dispensed justice, and accommodated differences. Cæs. ibid. c. 23. Their Kings had not absolute or unbounded power; their authority consisted rather in the privilege of advising, than in the power of commanding. Matters of small consequence were determined by the chief men; affairs of importance by the whole community. Tacit. c. 7, 11. The Huns, in like manner, deliberated in common concerning every business of moment to the society; and were not subject to the rigour of regal authority. Amm. Marcel. lib. xxxi. p. 474. (3) Every individual among the ancient Germans was left at liberty to chuse whether he would take part in any military enterprize which was proposed; there seems to have been no obligation to engage in it imposed on him by publick authority. "When any of the chief men proposes any expedition, such as approve of the cause and of the leader rise up and declare their intention of following him; and those who do not fulfil this engagement, are considered as deserters and traitors, and are looked upon as infamous." Cæs. ibid. c. 23. Tacitus plainly points at the same custom, though in terms more obscure. Tacit. c. 11. (4) As every individual was so independant, and master in so great a degree of his own actions, it became, of consequence, the great object of every person among the Germans who aimed at being a leader, to gain adherents, and attach them to his person and interest. These adherents Cæsar calls *Ambacti* and *Clientes*, i. e. retainers or clients; Tacitus, *Comites*, or companions. The chief distinction and power of the leaders, consisted in being attended by a numerous band of chosen youth. This was their pride as well as ornament during peace, and their defence in war. The favour of these retainers the leaders gained or preserved by presents of armour, and of horses; or by the profuse, though inelegant hospitality, with which they entertained them. Tacit. c. 14, 15. (5) Another consequence of the personal liberty and independance which the Germans retained, even after they united in society, was their circumscribing the criminal jurisdiction of the magistrate within very narrow limits, and their not only claiming but exercising almost all the rights of private resentment and revenge. Their magistrates had not the power either of imprisoning, or of inflicting any corporal punishment on a free man. Tacit. c. 7. Every person was obliged to avenge the wrongs which his parents or friends had sustained. Their enmities were hereditary, but not irreconcileable. Even murder was compensated by paying a certain number of cattle. Tac. c. 21. A part of the fine went to the King, or state, a part to the person who had been injured, or to his kindred. Ibid. c. 12.

These particulars concerning the institutions and manners of the Germans, though well known to every person conversant in ancient literature, I have thought proper to arrange in this order, and to lay before such of my readers as may be less acquainted with these facts, both because they confirm the account which I have given of the state of the barbarous nations, and tend to illustrate all the observations that I shall have occasion to make concerning the various changes in their government and customs. The laws and customs introduced by the barbarous nations into their new settlements, are the best commentary on the writings of Cæsar and Tacitus; and their observations are the best key to a perfect knowledge of these laws and customs.

One circumstance with respect to the testimonies of Cæsar and Tacitus concerning the Germans, merits attention. Cæsar wrote his brief account of their manners more than an hundred years before Tacitus composed his treatise de moribus Germanorum. An hundred years make a considerable period in the progress of national manners, especially if, during that time, those people who are rude and unpolished have had much communication with more civilized states. This was the case with the Germans. Their intercourse with the Romans began when Cæsar crossed the Rhine, and increased prodigiously during the interval between that event and the time when Tacitus flourished. Besides this, there was a considerable difference between the state of society among the different tribes of Germans. The Suiones were so much improved, that they began to be corrupted. Tac. cap. 44. The Fenni were so barbarous, that it is wonderful how they were able to subsist. Ibid. cap. 46. Whoever undertakes to describe the manners of the Germans, or to found any political theory upon the state of society among them, ought carefully to attend to both these circumstances.

Before I quit this subject, it may not be improper to observe, that though successive alterations in their institutions, together with the gradual progress of refinement, have made an entire change in the manners of the various people, who conquered the Roman Empire, there is still one race of men nearly in the same political situation with that in which they were when they first settled in their new conquests: I mean the various tribes and nations of Savages in North America. It cannot then be considered either as a digression, or as an improper indulgence of curiosity to enquire, whether this similarity in their political state has occasioned any resemblance between their character and manners. If the likeness turns out to be striking, it is a stronger proof that a just account has been given of the ancient inhabitants of Europe, than the testimony even of Cæsar or of Tacitus.

(1.) The Americans subsist chiefly by hunting and fishing. Some tribes neglect agriculture entirely. Among those who cultivate some small spot near their huts, that, together with all works of labour, is performed by the women. P. Charlevoix Journal Historique d'un Voyage de L'Amerique 4⁰. Par. 1744. p. 334. In such a state of society, the common wants of men being few, and their mutual dependence upon each other small, their union is extremely imperfect and feeble, and they continue to enjoy their natural liberty almost unimpaired. It is the first idea of an American, that every man is born free and independant, and that no power on earth hath any right to diminish or circumscribe his natural liberty. There is scarce any appearance of subordination either in civil or domestic government. Every one does what he pleases. A father and mother with their children, live like persons whom chance has brought together, and whom no common bond unites. Their manner of educating their children is suitable to this principle. They never chastise or punish them, even during their infancy. As they advance in years, they allow them to be entirely masters of their own actions, and responsible to no body. Id. p. 272, 273. (2.) The power of their civil magistrates is extremely limited. Among most of their tribes, the Sachem or chief is elective. A council of old men is chosen to assist him, without whose advice he determines no affair of importance. The Sachems neither possess nor claim any great degree of authority. They propose and intreat rather than command. The obedience of their people is altogether voluntary. Id. p. 266, 268. (3.) They engage in any military enterprize, not from constraint, but choice. When war is resolved, a chief arises, and offers himself to be the leader. They who are willing (for they compel no person) stand up one after another, and sing their war song. But if after this, any of these should refuse to follow the leader, to whom they have engaged, his life would be in danger, and he would be considered as the most infamous of all men. Id. p. 217, 218. (4.) Such as engage to follow any leader, expect to be treated by him with great attention and respect; and he is obliged to make them presents of considerable value. Id. p. 218. (5.) Among the Americans, the magistrate has scarce any criminal jurisdiction. Id. 272. Upon receiving any injury, the person or family offended may inflict what punishment they please on the person who was the author of it. Id. p. 274. Their resentment and desire of vengeance are excessive and implacable. Time can neither extinguish or abate it. It is the chief inheritance parents leave to their children; it is transmitted from generation to generation, until an occasion be found of satisfying it. Id. p. 309. Sometimes, however, the offended party is appeased. A compensation is paid for a murder that has been committed. The relations of the deceased receive it; and it consists most commonly of a captive taken in war, who being substituted in place of the person who was murdered, assumes his name, and is adopted into his family. Id. p. 274. The resemblance holds in many other particulars. It is sufficient for my purpose to have pointed out the similarity of those great features which distinguish and characterize both people. Bochart, and other philologists of the last century, who, with more erudition than science, endeavoured to trace the migrations of various nations, and who were apt, upon the slightest appearance of resemblance, to find an affinity between nations far removed from each other, and to conclude that they were descended from the same ancestors, would hardly have failed, on viewing such an amazing similarity, to pronounce with confidence, "That the Germans and Americans must be the same people." But a philosopher will satisfy himself with observing, "That the characters of nations depends on the state of society in which they live, and on the political institutions established among them; and that the human mind, whenever it is placed in the same situation, will, in ages the most distant, and in countries the most remote, assume the same form, and be distinguished by the same manners."

[Note to p. 17: On the Establishment of Feudalism in Europe]

The history of the establishment and progress of the feudal system, is an interesting object to all the nations of Europe. In some countries, their jurisprudence and laws are still in a great measure feudal. In others, many forms and practices established by custom, or founded on statutes, took their rise from the feudal law, and cannot be understood without attending to the ideas peculiar to it. Several authors of the highest reputation for genius and erudition, have endeavoured to illustrate this subject, but they have left many parts of it obscure. I shall endeavour to trace, with precision, the progress and variation of ideas concerning property in land among the barbarous nations; and shall attempt to point out the causes which introduced these changes, as well as the effects which followed upon them. Property in land seems to have gone through four successive changes among the people who settled in the various provinces of the Roman Empire.

I. While the barbarous nations remained in their original countries, they had no fixed property in land, and no certain limits to their possessions. After feeding their flocks in one district, they removed with them, their wives and families, to another; and abandoned that likewise in a short time. They were not, in consequence of this imperfect species of property, brought under any positive or formal obligation to serve the community; all their services were purely voluntary. Every individual was at liberty to chuse how far he would contribute towards carrying on any military enterprize. If he followed a leader in any expedition, it was from attachment, not from a sense of obligation. The clearest proof of this has been produced in [the preceding note]. While property continued in this state, we can discover nothing that bears any resemblance to a feudal tenure, or to the subordination and military service which the feudal system introduced.

II. Upon settling in the countries which they subdued, the victorious army divided the conquered lands. That portion which fell to every soldier, he seized as a recompence due to his valour, as a settlement acquired by his own sword. He took possession of it as a freeman in full property. He enjoyed it during his own life, and could dispose of it at pleasure, or transmit it as an inheritance to his children. Thus property in land became fixed. It was at the same time *allodial,* i.e. the possessor had the entire right of property and dominion; he held of no sovereign or superior lord, to whom he was bound to do homage, and perform service. But as these new proprietors were in some danger (as has been observed in the text) of being disturbed by the remainder of the ancient inhabitants, and in still greater danger of being attacked by barbarians as fierce and rapacious as themselves, they saw the necessity of coming under obligations to defend the community, more explicit than those to which they had been subject in their original habitations. On this account, immediately upon their fixing in their new settlements, every freeman became bound to take arms in defence of the community, and if he refused or neglected so to do, was liable to a considerable penalty. I do not mean that any contract of this kind was formally concluded, or mutually ratified by any legal solemnity. It was, like the other compacts which hold society together, established by tacit consent; and their mutual security and preservation made it the interest of all to recognize its authority and to enforce the observation of it. We can trace back this new obligation on the proprietors of land to a very early period in the history of the Franks. Chilperic, who began his reign A.D. 562, exacted a fine, *bannos jussit exigi,* from certain persons who had refused to accompany him in an expedition. Gregor. Turon. lib. v. c. 26. p. 211. Childibert, who began his reign A.D. 576, proceeded in the same manner against others who had been guilty of a like crime. Id. lib. vii. c. 42. p. 342. Charlemagne ordained, that every freeman who possessed five mansi, i.e. sixty acres of land, *in property,* should march in person against the enemy. Capitul. A.D. 807. Louis le Debonnaire, A.D. 815, granted lands to certain Spaniards who fled from the Saracens, and allowed them to settle in his territories, on condition that they should serve in the army *like other free men.* Capitul. vol. i. p. 500. By land possessed *in property,* which is mentioned in the law of Charlemagne, we are to understand, according to the stile of that age, allodial land; *allodes* and *proprietas, alodum* and *proprium* being words perfectly synonimous. Du Cange voce Alodis. The clearest proof of the distinction between allodial and beneficiary possession, is contained in two charters published by Muratori, by which it appears that a person might possess one part of his estate as allodial which he could dispose of at pleasure, the other as a beneficium, of which he had only the usufruct, the property returning to the superior Lord on his demise. Antiq. Ital. mediævi, vol. i. p. 559, 565. The same distinction is pointed out in a Capitulare of Charlemagne, A.D. 812, edit. Baluz. vol. p. 491. In the curious testament of count Everard, who married a daughter of Louis le Debonnaire, by which he disposes of his vast estate among his children, he distinguishes between what he possesses *proprietate,* and what he held *beneficio,* and it appears that the greater part was allodial. A.D. 837. Aub. Miræi Opera Diplomatica Lovan. 1723. Vol. p. 19.

In the same manner *Liber homo* is commonly opposed to *Vassus* or Vassallus; the former denotes an allodial proprietor, the latter one who held of a superior. These *free* men were under an obligation to serve the state; and this duty was considered as so sacred, that free men were prohibited from entering into holy orders unless they had obtained the consent of the sovereign. The reason given for this in the statute is remarkable, "For we are informed that some do so, not so much out of devotion, as in order to avoid that military service which they are bound to perform. Capitul. lib. i. §. 114. If upon being summoned into the field, any free man refused to obey, a full *Herebannum,* i.e. a fine of sixty crowns, was to be exacted from him according to the law of the Franks." Capit. Car. magn. ap. Leg. Longob. lib. i. tit. 14. §. 13. p. 539. This expression, according to the law of the Franks, seems to imply that both the obligation to serve, and the penalty on those who disregarded it, were coëval with the laws made by the Franks at their first settlement in Gaul. This fine was levied with such rigour, "That if any person was insolvent, he was reduced to servitude, and continued in that state until such time as his labour should amount to the value of the *herebannum.*" Ibid. The Emperor Lotharius rendered the penalty still more severe; and if any person possessing such an extent of property as made it incumbent on him to take the field in person refused to obey the summons, all his goods were declared to be forfeited, and he himself might be punished with banishment. Murat. Script. Ital. vol. i. pars ii. p. 153.

III. Property in land having thus become fixed and subject to military service, another change was introduced, though slowly, and step by step. We learn from Tacitus that the chief men among the Germans endeavoured to attach to their persons and interests certain adherents, whom he calls *Comites.* These fought under their standard, and followed them in all their enterprizes. The same custom continued among them in their new settlements, and those attached or devoted followers were called *fideles, antrustiones, homines in truste Dominica & leudes.* Tacitus informs us, that the rank of a Comes was deemed honourable; De morib. Germ. c. 13. The composition, which is the standard by which we must judge of the rank and condition of persons in the middle ages, paid for the murder of one *in truste Dominica,* was triple to that paid for the murder of a freeman. Leg. Salicor. Tit. 44. §. 1. & 2. While the Germans remained in their own country they courted the favour of these Comites by presents of arms and horses, and by hospitality. See [preceding note]. While they had no fixed property in land, these were the only gifts that they could bestow, and the only reward which their followers desired. But upon their settling in the countries which they conquered, and when the value of property came to be understood among them, instead of these slight presents, the Kings and chieftains bestowed a more substantial recompence in land on their adherents. These grants were called *beneficia*, because they were gratuitous donations; and *honores*, because they were regarded as marks of distinction. What were the services originally exacted in return for these *beneficia* cannot be determined with absolute precision; because there are no records so ancient. When allodial possessions were first rendered feudal, they were not, at once, subjected to the feudal services. The transition here, as in all other changes of importance, was gradual. As the great object of a feudal vassal was to obtain protection, when allodial proprietors first consented to become vassals of any powerful leader, they continued to retain as much of their ancient independance as was consistent with that new relation. The homage which they did to the superior of whom they chose to hold, was called *homagium planum,* and bound them to nothing more than fidelity, but without any obligation either of military service, or attendance in the courts of their superior. Of this *homagium planum* some traces, though obscure, may still be discovered. Brussel, tom. i. p. 97. Among the antient writs published by D. D. De Vic & Vaisette Hist. de Langued. are a great many which they call homagia. They seem to be an intermediate step between the homagium planum mentioned by Brussel, and the engagement to perform compleat feudal service. The one party promises protection, and grants certain castles or lands, the other engages to defend the person of the granter, and to assist him likewise in defending his property as often as he shall be summoned to do so. But these engagements are accompanied with none of the feudal formalities, and no mention is made of any of the feudal services. They appear rather to be a mutual contract between equals, than the engagement of a vassal to perform services to a superior Lord. Preuves de l'hist. de Lang. tom. ii. 173. & passim. As soon as men were accustomed to these, the other feudal services were gradually introduced. M.

de Montesquieu considers these *beneficia* as fiefs, which originally subjected those who held them to military service. L'espr. des Loix. 1. xxx. c. 3. & 16. M. l'abbè de Mably contends that such as held these were at first subjected to no other service than what was incumbent on every free man. Observations sur l'histoire de France I. 356. But upon comparing their proofs and reasonings and conjectures, it seems to be evident, that as every free man, in consequence of his allodial property, was bound to serve the community under a severe penalty, no good reason can be assigned for conferring these beneficia, if they did not subject such as received them, to some new obligation. Why should a King have stripped himself of his domain, if he had not expected, that, by parcelling it out, he might acquire a right to services to which he had formerly no title? We may then warrantably conclude, "That as allodial property subjected those who possessed it to serve the community, so *beneficia* subjected such as held them, to personal service and fidelity to him from whom they received these lands." These beneficia were granted originally only during pleasure. No circumstance relating to the customs of the middle ages is better ascertained than this; and innumerable proofs of it might be added to these produced in L'esprit des Loix, l. xxx. c. 16. and by Du Cange voc. *beneficium & feudum.*

IV. But the possession of benefices did not continue long in this state. A precarious tenure during pleasure was not sufficient to satisfy and attach those who held it to their superior Lord, they soon obtained the confirmation of their benefices during life. Feudor. lib. tit. i. Du Cange produces several quotations from ancient charters and chronicles in proof of this; Glos. voc. *Beneficium.* After this it was easy to obtain or extort charters rendering beneficia hereditary, first in the direct line, then in the collateral, and at last in the female line. Leg. Longob. lib. iii. tit. 8. Du Cange, voc. *Beneficium.*

It is no easy matter to fix the precise time when each of these changes took place. M. l'abbè de Mably conjectures with some probability, that Charles Martel first introduced the practice of granting beneficia for life: Observat. tom. i. p. 103, 160; and that Louis le Debonnaire was among the first who rendered them hereditary, is evident from the authorities to which he refers; Id. 429. Mabillon however has published a placitum of Louis le Debonnaire. A.D. 860. by which it appears that he still continued to grant some beneficia only during life. De re Diplomatica, lib. vi. p. 353. In the year 889, Odo King of France granted lands to Ricabodo fideli suo jure beneficiario & fructuario during his own life; and if he should die, and a son were born to him, that right was to continue during the life of his son. Mabillon ut supra, p. 556. This was an intermediate step between fiefs merely during life, and fiefs hereditary to perpetuity. While beneficia continued under their first form, and were held only during pleasure, he who granted them not only exercised the *Dominium* or prerogative of superior Lord; but he retained the property, giving his vassal only the *usufruct*. But under the latter form, when they became hereditary, although feudal lawyers continued to define a beneficium agreeably to its original nature, the property was in effect taken out of the hands of the superior Lord, and lodged in those of the vassal. As soon as the reciprocal advantages of the feudal mode of tenure came to be understood by superiors as well as vassals, that species of holding became so agreeable to both, that not only lands, but casual rents, such as the profits of a toll, the fare paid at ferries, &c. the salaries or perquisites of offices, and even pensions themselves, were granted and held as fiefs; and military service was promised and exacted on account of these. Morice Mem. pour servir de preuves a l'hist. de Bretagne. tom. ii. 78. 690. Brussel, tom. i. p. 41. How absurd soever it may seem to grant or to hold such precarious and casual property as a fief; there are instances of feudal tenures still more singular. The profits arising from the masses said at an altar were properly an ecclesiastical revenue, belonging to the clergy of the church or monastery which performed that duty, but these were sometimes seized by the powerful barons. In order to ascertain their right to them, they held them as fiefs of the church, and parcelled them out in the same manner as other property to their subvassals. Bouquet Recueil des hist. vol. x. 238. 480. The same spirit of encroachment which rendered fiefs hereditary, led the nobles to extort from their sovereigns hereditary grants of offices. Many of the great offices of the crown became hereditary in most of the kingdoms in Europe, and so conscious were monarchs of this spirit of usurpation among the nobility, and so sollicitous to guard against it, that, on some occasions, they obliged the persons whom they promoted to any office of dignity, to grant an obligation that neither they, nor their heirs, should claim it as belonging to them by hereditary right. A remarkable instance of this is produced, Mem. de l'Acad. des Inscript. tom. xxx. p. 595. Another occurs in the Thesaur. anecdot. published by Martène & Durand. vol. i. p. 873. This revolution in property occasioned a change corresponding to it in political government; the great vassals of the crown, as they acquired such extensive possessions, usurped a proportional degree of power, depressed the jurisdiction of the crown, and trampled on the privileges of the people. It is on account of this connection, that the tracing the progress of feudal property becomes an object of attention in history; for upon discovering in what state property was at any particular period, we may determine with precision what was the degree of power possessed by the King or by the nobility at that juncture.

One circumstance more, with respect to the changes which property underwent, deserves attention. I have shewn that when the various tribes of barbarians divided their conquests in the fifth and sixth centuries, the property which they acquired was allodial; but in several parts of Europe property had become almost entirely feudal by the beginning of the tenth century. The former species of property seems to be so much better and more desirable than the latter, that such a change appears surprising, especially when we are informed that allodial property was frequently converted into feudal, by a voluntary deed of the possessor. The motives which determined them to a choice so repugnant to the ideas of modern times concerning property, have been investigated and explained by M. de Montesquieu with his usual discernment and accuracy, lib. xxxi. c. 8. The most considerable is that of which we have an hint in Lambertus Ardensis, an ancient writer quoted by Du Cange, voce *Alodis*. In those times of anarchy and disorder which became general in Europe after the death of Charlemagne; when there was scarce any union among the different members of the community; and individuals were exposed, single and undefended by government, to rapine and oppression, it became necessary for every man to have a powerful protector, under whose banner he might range himself, and obtain security against enemies, whom he could not singly oppose. For this reason he relinquished his allodial independance, and subjected himself to the feudal services, that he might find safety under the patronage of some respectable superior. In some parts of Europe, this change from allodial to feudal property became so general, that he who possessed land had no longer any liberty of choice left. He was obliged to recognize some liege Lord, and to hold of him. Thus Beaumanoir informs us, that in the counties of Clermont and Beauvois, if the Lord or Count discovered any lands within his jurisdiction, for which no service was performed, and which paid to him no tax or customs, he might instantly seize it as his own; for, says he, according to our custom no man can hold allodial property. Coust. ch. 24. p. 123. Upon the same principle is founded a maxim, which has at length become general in the law of France, *Nulle terre sans Seigneur.* In other provinces of France allodial property seems to have remained longer unalienated, and to have been more highly valued. A vast number of charters containing grants, or sales, or exchanges of allodial lands in the province of Languedoc are published Hist. gener. de Langued. par D. D. De Vic & Vaisette, tom. ii. During the ninth, tenth, and greater part of the eleventh century, the property in that province seems to have been entirely allodial; and scarce any mention of feudal tenures occurs in the deeds of that country. The state of property, during these centuries, seems to have been perfectly similar in Catalonia, and the country of Roussillon, as appears from the original charters published in the appendix to Petr. de la Marca's treatise De Marca Sive limite Hispanico. Allodial property seems to have continued in the Low-Countries, to a period still later. During the eleventh, twelfth, and thirteenth centuries, this species appears to have been of considerable extent. Miræi Opera Diplom. vol. i. 34, 74, 75, 83, 817, 296, 842, 847, 578. Some vestiges of allodial property appear there as late as the fourteenth century. Ibid. 218. The notions of men with respect to property, vary according to the diversity of their understandings, and the caprice of their passions. At the same time that some persons were fond of relinquishing allodial property, in order to hold it by feudal tenure, others seem to have been sollicitous to convert their fiefs into allodial property. An instance of this occurs in a charter of Louis le Debonnaire, published by Eckhard, commentarii de rebus Franciæ Orientalis, vol. ii. 885. Another occurs in the year 1299. Reliquiæ MSS. omnis ævi, by Ludwig, vol. i. p. 209. and even one as late as the year 1337. ibid. vol. vii. p. 40. The same thing took place in the Low-Countries. Miraei oper. i. 52.

In tracing these various revolutions of property, I have hitherto chiefly confined myself to what happened in France, because the ancient monuments of that nation have either been more carefully preserved, or have been more clearly illustrated than those of any people in Europe.

In Italy, the same revolutions happened in property, and succeeded each other in the same order. There is some ground, however, for conjecturing that allodial property continued longer in estimation among the Italians, than among the French. It appears that many of the charters granted by the Emperors in the ninth century conveyed an allodial right to land. Murat. antiq. med. ævi. v. i. p. 575, &c. But in the eleventh century, we find some examples of persons who resigned their allodial property, and received it back as a feudal tenure. Ib. p. 610, &c. Muratori observes, that the word *feudum*, which came to be substituted in place of *beneficium*, does not occur in any authentick charter previous to the eleventh century. Id. 594. A charter of King Robert of France, A.D. 1008, is the earliest deed in which I have met with the word *feudum*. Bouquet Recueil des historiens de Gaule & de la France, tom. x. p. 593. b. This word occurs indeed in an edict, A.D. 790, published by Brussel, vol. i. p. 77. But the authenticity of that deed has been called in question, and perhaps the frequent use of the word *feudum* in it, is an additional reason for doing so. The account which I have given of the nature both of allodial and feudal possessions receives some confirmation from the etymology of the words themselves. *Alode* or *allodium* is compounded of the German particle *an* and *lot, i. e.* land obtained by lot. Wachteri Glossar. Germanicum, voc. *Allodium.* p. 35. It appears from the authorities produced by him and by Du Cange, voc. *sors,* that the northern nations divided the lands which they had conquered in this manner. Feodum is compounded of *od* possession or estate, and *feo* wages, pay; intimating that it was stipendiary and granted as a recompence for service. Wachterus ibid. voc. *feodum,* p. 441.

The progress of the feudal system among the Germans was perfectly similar to that which we have traced in France. But as the Emperors of Germany, especially after the Imperial crown passed from the descendants of Charlemagne to the house of Saxony, were far superior to the contemporary Monarchs of France, in abilities, the Imperial vassals did not aspire so early to independance, nor did they so soon obtain the privilege of possessing their benefices by hereditary right. Conrad II of the Salic, was the first Emperor, according to the compilers of the Libri Feudorum, who rendered fiefs hereditary. Lib. i. tit. i. Conrad began his reign A.D. 1024. Ludovicus Pius, under whose reign, grants of hereditary fiefs were frequent in France, succeeded his father, A.D. 814. Not only was this innovation so much later in being introduced among the vassals of the German Emperors, but even after Conrad had established it, the law continued favourable to the ancient practice, and unless the charter of the vassal bore expressly that the fief descended to his heirs, it was presumed to be granted only during life. Lib. feud. ibid. Even after the alteration made by Conrad, it was not uncommon in Germany to grant fiefs only for life; a charter of this kind occurs as late as the year 1376. Charta ap. Boehmer Princip. Jur. feud. p. 361. The transmission of fiefs to collateral and female heirs, took place very slowly among the Germans. There is extant a charter, A.D. 1201. conveying the right of succession to females, but it is granted as an extraordinary mark of favour, and in reward of uncommon services. Boehmer ibid. p. 365. In Germany, as well as in France and Italy, a considerable part of the lands continued to be allodial long after the feudal mode of tenure was introduced. It appears from the Codex Diplomaticus Monasterii Buch, that a great part of the lands in the marquisate of Misnia was still allodial as late as the thirteenth century. No. 31, 36, 37, 46, &c. ap. Scriptores hist. German. cura Schoetgenii & Kreysigii. Altenb. 1755. vol. ii. 183, &c. Allodial property seems to have been common in another district of the same province, during the same period. Reliquiæ Diplomaticæ Sanctimonial. Beutiz. No. 17, 36, 58. ibid. 374, &c.

[Note to p. 67: On the Beginnings of Commerce]
The great variety of subjects which I have endeavoured to illustrate, and the extent of this upon which I now enter, will justify my adopting the words of M. de Montesquieu, when he begins to treat of commerce. "The subject which follows would require to be discussed more at large; but the nature of this work does not permit it. I wish to glide on a tranquil stream; but I am hurried along by a torrent."

Many proofs occur in history of the little intercourse between nations during the middle ages. Toward the close of the tenth century, Count Bouchard intending to found a monastery at St. Maur des Fosses, near Paris, applied to an abbot of Clugny in Burgundy, famous for his sanctity, intreating him to conduct the monks thither. The language in which he addressed that holy man is singular: He tells him, that he had undertaken the labour of such a great journey; that he was fatigued with the length of it, therefore hoped to obtain his request, and that his journey into such a distant country should not be in vain. The answer of the abbott is still more extraordinary: He refused to comply with his desire, as it would be extremely fatiguing to go along with him into a strange and unknown region. Vita Burchardi venerabilis Comitis ap. Bouquet Rec. des. Hist. vol. x. p. 351. Even so late as the beginning of the twelfth century, the monks of Ferrieres in the diocese of Sens did not know that there was such a city as Tournay in Flanders; and the monks of St. Martin of Tournay were equally unacquainted with the situation of Ferrieres. A transaction in which they were both concerned, made it necessary for them to have some intercourse. The mutual interest of both monasteries prompted each to find out the situation of the other.

After a long search, which is particularly described, the discovery was made by accident. Herimannus Abbas de Restauratione St. Martini Tornacensis ap. Dacher. Spicel. vol. xii. p. 400. The ignorance of the middle ages with respect to the situation and geography of remote countries was still more remarkable. The most ancient geographical chart which now remains as a monument of the state of that science in Europe during the middle ages, is found in a manuscript of the Chronique de St. Denys. There the three parts of the earth then known are so represented, that Jerusalem is placed in the middle of the globe, and Alexandria appears to be as near to it as Nazareth. Mem. de l'Acad. des Belles Lettres, tom. xvi. p. 185. There seem to have been no inns or houses of entertainment for the reception of travellers during the middle ages. Murat. Antiq. Ital. vol. iii. p. 581 &c. This is a proof of the little intercourse which took place between different nations. Among people whose manners are simple, and who are seldom visited by strangers, hospitality is a virtue of the first rank. This duty of hospitality was so necessary in that state of society which took place during the middle ages, that it was not considered as one of those virtues which men may practice or not, according to the temper of their minds, and the generosity of their hearts. Hospitality was enforced by statutes, and those who neglected this duty were liable to punishment. Quicumque hospiti venienti lectum, aut focum negaverit, trium selidorum inlatione mulctetur, Leg. Burgund. tit. xxxviii. § 1. Si quis homini aliquo pergenti in itinere mansionem vetaverit sexaginta solidos componat in publico. Capitul. lib .vi. § 82. This increase of the penalty, at a period so long after that in which the laws of the Burgundians were published, and when the state of society was much improved, is very remarkable. Other laws of the same purport are collected by Jo. Fred. Polæ Systema Jurisprud. Germanicæ, Lips. 1733. p. 75. The laws of the Slavi were more rigorous than any that he mentions; they ordained, "that the moveables of an inhospitable person should be confiscated, and his house burnt. They were even so sollicitous for the entertainment of strangers, that they permitted the landlord to steal for the support of his guest." Quod noctu furatus fueris, cras appone, hospitibus.

Rerum Mecleburgicar. lib. viii. a Mat. Jo. Beehr. Lips. 1751. p. 50. In consequence of these laws, or of that state of society which made it proper to enact them, hospitality abounded while the inter course among men was inconsiderable, and secured the stranger a kind reception under every roof where he chose to take shelter. This, too, proves clearly, that the intercourse among men was rare, for as soon as this increased, what was a pleasure became burden, and the entertaining of travellers was converted into a branch of commerce.

But the laws of the middle ages afford a proof still more convincing of the small intercourse between different nations. The genius of the feudal system, as well as the spirit of jealousy which always accompanies ignorance, joined in discouraging strangers from settling in any country. If a person removed from one province in a kingdom to another, he was bound within a year and a day to acknowledge himself the vassal of the baron in whose estate he settled; if he neglected to do so, he became liable to a penalty; and if at his death he neglected to leave a certain legacy to the baron within whose territories he resided, all his goods were confiscated. The hardships imposed on foreigners settling in a strange country, were still more intolerable. In more early times, the superior lord of any territory in which a foreigner settled, might seize his person, and reduce him to servitude. Very striking instances of this occur in the history of the middle ages. The cruel depredations of the Normans in the ninth century, obliged many inhabitants of the maritime provinces of France to fly into the interior parts of the kingdom. But instead of being received with that humanity to which their wretched condition entitled them, they were reduced to a state of servitude. Both the civil and ecclesiastical powers found it necessary to interpose, in order to put a stop to this barbarous practice. Potgiesser. de Statu Servor. i. c. i. § 16. In other countries, the laws permitted the inhabitants of the maritime provinces to reduce such as were shipwrecked on their coast to servitude. Ibid. § 17. This barbarous custom prevailed in other countries of Europe. The practice of seizing the goods of persons who had been shipwrecked, and of confiscating as the property of the lord on whose manor they were thrown, seems to have been universal. De Westphalen Monum. inedita Rer. Germ. vol iv. p. 907, &c. et Du Cange, voc. *Laganum*, Beehr. Rer. Mecleb. lib. p. 512. Among the ancient Welsh, three sorts of persons, a madman, a stranger, and a leper, might be killed with impunity. Leges Hoel Dda, quoted in Observat. on the Statutes, chiefly the more ancient, p. 22. M. de Lauriere produces several ancient deeds which prove that in different provinces of France, strangers became the slaves of the lord on whose lands they settled. Glossaire du Droit Francois, Art. *Aubaine*, p. 92. Beaumanoir says, "that there are several places in France, in which if a stranger fixes his residence for a year and day, he becomes the slave of the lord of the manor. Coust. de Beauv. ch. 45. p. 254. But as a practice so contrary to humanity could not subsist, the superior lords found it necessary to rest satisfied with levying certain annual taxes from aliens, imposing upon them some extraordinary duties or services. But when any stranger died, he could not convey his effects by a will; and all his real as well as personal estate fell to the King, or to the lord of the barony, to the exclusion of his natural heirs. This is termed in France Droit d'Aubaine. Pref. de Laurier. Ordon. tom. i. p. 15. Brussel. tom. ii. p. 944. Du Cange, voc. *Albani*. Pasquier Recherches, p. 367. This practice of confiscating the effects of strangers upon their death was very ancient. It is mentioned, though very obscurely, in a law of Charlemagne, A. D. 813. Capitul. Baluz. p. 507. § 5. Not only persons who were born in a foreign country were subject to the Droit d'Aubaine, but even such as removed from one diocese to another, or from the lands of one baron to another. Brussel. vol. ii. p. 947, 949. It is scarce possible to conceive any law more unfavourable to the intercourse between nations. Something similar to it, however, may be found in the ancient laws of every kingdom in Europe. With respect to Italy, see Murat. Ant. vol. ii. p. 14. It is no small disgrace to the French jurisprudence, that this barbarous, inhospitable custom, should still remain in a nation so highly civilized.

The confusion and outrage which abounded under a feeble form of government, incapable of framing or executing salutary

laws, rendered the communication between the different provinces of the same kingdom extremely dangerous. It appears
from a letter of Lupus, abbot of Ferrieres, in the ninth century,
that the highways were so much infested by banditti, that it was
necessary for travellers to form themselves into companies or
caravans, that they might be safe from the assaults of robbers.
Bouquet Recueil des Hist. vol. vii. 515. The numerous regulations published by Charles the Bald in the same century, discover the frequency of these disorders; and such acts of violence
were become so common, that by many they were hardly considered as criminal; and for this reason the inferior judges called
Centenarii were required to take an oath, that they would
neither commit any robbery themselves, nor protect such as were
guilty of that crime. Capitul. edit. Baluz. vol. ii. p. 63, 68.
The historians of the ninth and tenth centuries give pathetic
descriptions of these disorders. Some remarkable passages to
this purpose are collected by Mat. Jo. Beehr Rer. Mecleb. lib.
viii. p. 603. They became so frequent and audacious, that the
authority of the civil magistrate was unable to repress them.
The ecclesiastical jurisdiction was called in to aid it. Councils
were held with great solemnity, the bodies of the saints were
brought thither, and in presence of their sacred reliques, anathemas were denounced against robbers, and other violators of
the publick peace. Bouquet Recueil des Hist. tom. x. p. 360, 431,
536. One of these forms of excommunication issued A. D. 988, is
still preserved, and is so singular, and composed with eloquence
of such a peculiar kind, that it will not perhaps appear unworthy
of a place here. After the usual introduction, and mentioning
the outrage which gave occasion to the anathema, it runs thus:
"Obtenebrescant occuli vestri, qui concupiverunt; arescant
manus, quæ rapuerunt; debilitentur omnia membra, quæ ad-
juverunt. Semper laboretis, nec requiem inveniatis, fructuque
vestri laboris privemini. Formidetis, & paveatis, à facie persequentis, & non persequentis hostis, ut tabescendo deficiatis. Sit
portio vestra cum Juda traditore Domini, in terra mortis et
tenebrarum; donec corda vestra ad satisfactionem plenam con-
vertantur.—Ne cessent a vobis hæ malidictiones, scelerum ves-

trorum persecutrices, quamdiu permanebitis in peccato pervasionis. Amen. Fiat, Fiat." Bouquet. Ib. p. 517.

With respect to the progress of commerce which I have described, p. 63, &c. it may be observed that the Italian states carried on some commerce with the cities of the Greek empire, as early as the age of Charlemagne, and imported into their own country the rich commodities of the east. Murat. Antiq. Ital. vol. ii. p. 882. In the tenth century, the Venetians had opened a trade with Alexandria in Egypt. Ibid. The inhabitants of Amalphi and Pisa had likewise extended their trade to the same ports. Murat. Ib. p. 884, 885. The effects of the Crusades in increasing the wealth and commerce of the Italian states, and particularly that which they carried on with the East, I have explained page 27th of this volume. They not only imported the Indian commodities from the East, but estblished manufactures of curious fabric in their own country. Several of these are enumerated by Muratori in his Differtations concerning the *arts* and the *weaving* of the middle ages. Antiq. Ital. vol. ii. p. 349, 399. They made great progress, particularly in the manufacture of silk, which had long been peculiar to the eastern provinces of Asia. Silk stuffs were of such high price in ancient Rome, that only a few persons of the first rank were able to purchase them. Under Aurelian, A. D. 270, a pound of silk was equal in value to a pound of gold. Absit ut auro fila pensentur. Libra enim auri tunc libra serici fuit. Vopiscus in Aureliano. Justinian, in the sixth century, introduced the art of rearing silk-worms into Greece, which rendered the commodity somewhat more plentiful, though still it was of such great value, as to remain an article of luxury or magnificence, reserved only for persons of the first order, or for publick solemnities. Roger I King of Sicily, about the year 1130, carried off a number of artificers in the silk trade from Athens, and settling them in Palermo, introduced the culture of silk into his kingdom, from which it was communicated to other parts of Italy. Gianon. Hist. of Naples, b. xi. c. 7. This seems to have rendered silk so common, that about the middle of the fourteenth century, a thousand citizens of Genoa, appeared in one procession clad in silk robes.

Sugar is likewise a production of the East. Some plants of the sugar cane were brought from Asia; and the first attempt to cultivate them in Sicily was made about the middle of the twelfth century. From thence they were transplanted into the southern provinces of Spain. From Spain they were carried to the Canary and Madeira isles, and at length into the new world. Ludovico Guicciardini, in enumerating the goods imported into Antwerp, about the year 1560, mentions the sugar which they received from Spain and Portugal as a considerable article. He describes that as the product of the Madeira and Canary islands. Descritt. de Paesi Bassi, p. 180, 181. The sugar cane was either not introduced into the West-Indies at that time, or the cultivation of it was not so considerable as to furnish an article in commerce. In the middle ages, though sugar was not raised in such quantities, or employed for so many purposes, as to become one of the common necessaries of life, it appears to have been a considerable article in the commerce of the Italian states.

These various commodities with which the Italians furnished the other nations of Europe, procured them a favourable reception in every kingdom. They were established in France in the thirteenth century with most extensive immunities. They not only obtained every indulgence favourable to their commerce, but personal rights and privileges were granted to them, which the natives of the kingdom did not enjoy. Ordon. tom. iv. p. 668. By a special proviso, they were exempted from the droit d'aubaine. Ibid. p. 670. As the Lombards engrossed the trade of every kingdom in which they settled, they became masters of its cash. Money of course was in their hands not only a sign of the value of their commodities, but became an object of commerce itself. They dealt largely as bankers. In an ordonance, A.D. 1295, we find them stiled *mercatores* and *campsores*. They carried on this as well as other branches of their commerce with somewhat of that rapacious spirit which is natural to monopolizers, who are not restrained by the concurrence of rivals. An absurd opinion, which prevailed in the middle ages, was, however, in some measure, the cause of their exorbitant demands, and may be pleaded in apology for them. Commerce cannot be carried on with advantage unless the persons who lend a sum are allowed a certain premium for the use of their money, and as a compensation for the risk which they run in permitting another to traffick with their stock. This premium is fixed by law in all commercial countries, and is called the legal interest of money. But the Fathers of the church preposterously applied the prohibitions of usury in scripture to the payment of legal interest, and condemned it as a sin. The schoolmen, misled by Aristotle, whose sentiments they followed implicitly, and without examination, adopted the same error, and enforced it. Blackstone's Commentaries on the laws of England, vol. ii p. 455. Thus the Lombards found themselves engaged in a traffick which was deemed criminal and odious. They were liable to punishment if detected. They were not satisfied, therefore, with that moderate premium, which they might have claimed if their trade had been open and authorised by law. They exacted a sum proportional to the danger and infamy of a discovery. Accordingly, we find that it was usual for them to demand twenty per cent. for the use of money in the thirteenth century. Murat. Antiq. Ital. vol. i. p. 893. About the beginning of that century, the countess of Flanders was obliged to borrow money in order to pay her husband's ransom. She procured the sum requisite, either from Italian merchants or from Jews. The lowest interest which she paid to them was above twenty per cent. and some of them exacted near thirty. Martène and Durand, Thesaur. Anecdotorum. vol. i. p. 886. In the fourteenth century, A.D. 1311, Philip IV fixed the interest which might be legally exacted in the fairs of Champagne at twenty per cent. Ordonan. tom. i. p. 484. The interest of money in Aragon was somewhat lower. James I, A.D. 1242, fixed it by law at eighteen per cent. Petr. de Marca. *Marca* sive Limes Hispan. app. 1433. As late as the year 1490, it appears that the interest of money in Placentia, was at the rate of forty per cent. This is the more extraordinary, because at that time the commerce of the Italian States was become considerable. Memorie Storiche de Piacenza, tom. viii. p. 104. Piac. 1760. It appears from Lud. Guicciardini, that Charles V had fixed the rate of interest in his dominions in in the Low-Countries at twelve per cent, and at the time when he wrote about the year 1560, it was not uncommon to exact more than that sum. He complains of this as exorbitant, and points out its bad effects both on agriculture and commerce. Descritt. di Paesi Bassi, p. 172. This high interest of money, is alone a proof that the profits on commerce were exorbitant. The Lombards were likewise established in England, in the thirteenth century, and a considerable street in the city of London still bears their name. They enjoyed great privileges, and carried on an extensive commerce, particularly as bankers. See Anderson's Chronol. Deduction, vol. i. p. 137, 160, 204, 231, where the statutes or other authorities which confirm this are quoted. But the chief mart for Italian commodities was at Bruges. Navigation was then so imperfect, that a voyage between the Baltick and Mediterranean could not be performed in one summer. For that reason a magazine or storehouse half way between the commercial cities in the north, and those in Italy became necessary. Bruges was pitched upon as the most convenient station. That choice introduced vast wealth into the Low-Countries. Bruges was at once the staple for English wool; for the woollen and linen manufactures of the Netherlands; for the naval stores, and other bulky commodities of the north; and for the Indian commodities, as well as domestick productions imported by the Italian States. The extent of its commerce in Indian goods with Venice alone appears from one fact. In the year 1318, five Venetian galeasses laden with Indian commodities arrived at Bruges, in order to dispose of their cargoes at the fair. L. Guic. Descritt. di Paesi Bassi, p. 174. Galeasses were vessels of very considerable burden. It was the greatest emporium in all Europe. Many proofs of this occur in the historians and records of the thirteenth and fourteenth centuries. But instead of multiplying quotations, I shall refer my readers to Anderson, vol. i. p. 12, 137, 213, 246, &c. The nature of this work prevents me from entering into any long details, but there are some detached facts, which give an high idea of the wealth both of the Flemish and Italian commercial states. The Duke of Brabant contracted his daughter to the Black Prince, son of Edward III of England, A.D. 1339, and gave her a portion which would have amounted to three hundred thousand pounds of our

present money. Rymer's Fædera, vol. v. p. 113. John Galeazzo
Visconti Duke of Milan concluded a treaty of marriage between
his daughter and Lionel Duke of Clarence Edward's third son.
A.D. 1367. and granted her a portion equal to two hundred thousand pounds of our present money. Rymer Fæder. vol. vi. p. 547.
These exorbitant sums so far exceeding what was then granted
by the most powerful monarchs, and which appear extraordinary
even in the present age, when the wealth of Europe is so much
increased, must have arisen from the riches which flowed into
these countries from their extensive and lucrative commerce. The
first source of wealth to the towns situated on the Baltick sea,
seems to have been the herring-fishery; the shoals of herring fre-
quenting at that time the coasts of Sweden and Denmark, in the
same manner as they now resort to the British coasts. The effects
of this fishery are thus described by an author of the thirteenth
century. The Danes, says he, who were formerly clad in the poor
garb of sailors, are now cloathed in scarlet, purple and fine linen.
For they abound with wealth flowing from their annual fishery
on the coast of Schonen; so that all nations resort to them, bring-
ing their gold, silver and precious commodities, that they may
purchase herrings, which the divine bounty bestows upon them.
Arnoldus Lubecensis ap. Conring. de Urbib. German. § 87.

The Hanseatick league is the most powerful commercial confederacy known in history. Its origin towards the close of the
twelfth century, and the objects of its union, are described by
Knipseildt Tractatus Historico-Politico Juridicus de Juribus
Civitat. Imper. lib. i.cap. 4. Anderson has mentioned the chief
facts with respect to their commercial progress, the extent of the
privileges which they obtained in different countries, their successful wars with several monarchs, as well as the spirit and zeal
with which they contended for those liberties and rights without
which it is impossible to carry on commerce to advantage. The
vigorous efforts of a society attentive only to commercial objects,
could not fail of diffusing over Europe new and more liberal ideas
concerning justice and order wherever they settled.

In England the progress of commerce wes extremely slow; and
the causes of this are obvious. During the Saxon heptarchy,

England, split into many petty kingdoms, which were perpetually at variance with each other, exposed to the fierce incursions of the Danes, and other northern pirates, and sunk in barbarity and ignorance, was in no condition to cultivate commerce, or to pursue any system of useful and salutary policy. When a better prospect began to open by the union of the kingdom under one monarch, the Norman conquest took place. This occasioned such a violent shock, and such a sudden and total revolution of property, that the nation did not recover from it during several reigns. By the time that the constitution began to acquire some stability, and the English had so incorporated with their conquerors as to become one people, the nation engaged with no less ardour than imprudence in support of their monarch's pretensions to the crown of France, and long wasted its vigour and genius in its wild efforts to conquer that kingdom. When by ill success, and repeated disappointments, a period was at last put to this fatal frenzy, and the nation beginning to enjoy some repose, had leisure to breathe and to gather new strength, the destructive wars between the houses of York and Lancaster broke out, and involved the kingdom in the worst of all calamities. Thus, besides the common obstructions of commerce occasioned by the nature of the feudal government, and the state of manners during the middle ages, its progress in England was retarded by peculiar causes. Such a succession of events adverse to the commercial spirit was sufficient to have checked its growth, although every other circumstance had favoured it. The English were accordingly one of the last nations in Europe who availed themselves of their natural commercial advantages. Before the reign of Edward III all the wool of England, except a small quantity wrought into coarse cloths for home consumption, was sold to the Flemings or Lombards, and manufactured by them. Though Edward, A.D. 1326, began to allure some of the Flemish weavers to settle in England, it was long before the English were capable of fabricating cloth for foreign markets, and the export of unwrought wool still continued to be the chief article of their commerce. Anderson passim. All foreign commodities were brought into England by the Lombard or Hanseatick merchants. The English ports were frequented by ships from the north and south of Europe, and they tamely allowed foreigners to reap all the profits arising from the supply of their wants. The first commercial treaty of England on record, is that with Haquin King of Norway, A.D. 1217. Anders. vol. i. p. 108. But they did not venture to trade in their own ships to the Baltick until the beginning of the fourteenth century. Ib. 151. It was after the middle of the fifteenth before they sent any ship into the Mediterranean. Ib. p. 177. Nor was it long before this period that their vessels visited the ports of Spain or Portugal. But though I have pointed out the slow progress of the English commerce, as a fact little attended to, and yet meriting consideration; the concourse of foreigners to the ports of England, together with the communication among all the different countries in Europe, which went on increasing from the beginning of the twelfth century, is sufficient to justify all the observations and reasonings in the text concerning the influence of commerce on the state of manners, and of society.

Notes

I Interior Government, Laws and Manners

1. Theodosius died A.D. 395. The reign of Alboinus in Lombardy began A.D. 571, so that this period was 176 years.

2. Montesquieu, *De l'Esprit des Lois*, bk. 17, chap. 3.

3. Procopius, *De Bello Vandalico*, in Procopii Caesariensis *Opera* (Corpus Byzantinae Historiae) (Venice, 1729), 1:345.

4. Du Cange, *Glossarium Mediae et Infimae Latinitatis*, s.v. "Miles."

5. David Hume, *The History of England* (London, 1762), 2:441.

6. Rev. 20:2–4.

7. See Martin Bouquet, *Recueil des historiens des Gaules et de la France*, vol. 10, the chronicle of Willelmus Godellus, p. 262, and the Vita Abbonis, p. 332; see in *Corpus Historicum Medii Aevi*, ed. J. G. von Eckhart, vol. 1 (Leipzig, 1723), the chronicle of Pantaleon, p. 909, and the Annalista Saxo, p. 576.

8. See Foulcher of Chartres in *Gesta Dei per Francos, sive Orientalium Expeditionum . . . Historia*, ed. Jacques Bongars (Hannover, 1611), 1:387.

9. Anna Comnena, *Alexias* (Corpus Byzantinae Historiae), 11:224.

10. William of Malmesbury, Guibert de Nogent in *Gesta Dei*, 1:481.

11. Du Cange, *Glossarium*, s.v. "Cruce Signatus"; Gulielmus, Abbott of S. Benignus in Dijon, in *Gesta Dei*, 1:480–82.

12. Muratori, *Antiquitates Italicae Medii Aevi* (n.p., 1738), 2:905.

13. Muratori, *Antiquitates Italicae*, 2:906 ff.

14. Villehardouin (Geoffroy de), *Histoire de l'Empire de Constantinople sous les Empereurs François*, ed. Du Cange (Paris, 1657), pp. 105 ff.

15. See Achery (Luc d'), *Veterum aliquot scriptorum qui in Galliae Bibliotecis latuerant Spicilegium*, 11:374, 375; and see *Ordonnances des Roys de France de la Troisième Race* (Paris, 1733), 3:204.

16. *Ordonnances*, 1:22; 3:203; Muratori, *Antiquitates Italicae;* 4:20; Achery, *Spicilegium*, 11:325, 341.

17. Achery, *Spicilegium*, 9:182.

18. Mably (Bonnot de), *Observations sur l'Histoire de France* (Geneva, 1765), 2:2, 96.

19. Muratori, *Antiquitates Italicae*, 4:5.

20. Achery, *Spicilegium,* 9:182, 185, 193.

21. *Ordonnances,* 1:602, 785; 2:318, 422.

22. Pasquier (Etienne), *Les Recherches de la France* (Paris, 1633), p. 81.

23. Pfeffel von Kriegelstein (Christian Friedberg), *Abrégé chronologique de l'histoire et du droit public d'Allemange* (n.p., 1754), pp. 408, 451.

24. *Ordonnances,* 1:283.

25. *Ordonnances,* 1:583, 653.

26. Tacitus, *De moribus et populis Germanorum liber,* chap. 21.

27. Beaumanoir (Philippe de Remi), *Coustumes de Beauvoisis,* avec des notes par Gaspard Thaumas de la Thaumassière (Paris, 1690), chap. 59.

28. *Capitularia regum francorum ab anno 742 ad annum 922,* ed. Stephan Baluze (Paris, 1674), 1:371.

29. Leges Burgundionum, tit. 8 and 45, Leges Alemannerum, tit. 89, from *Corpus Juris Germanici Antiqui,* ed. Georgisch (Halle, 1738).

30. Du Cange, *Glossarium,* s.v. "Juramentum."

31. Ibid., 3:1599.

32. Spelman (Sir Henry), *Glossarium Archaiologicum* (London, 1664), s.v. "Assath."

33. Leges Langobardorum, bk. 2, tit. 55, par. 34.

34. Muratori, *Antiquitates Italicae,* 3:612.

35. See a curious discourse concerning the laws of judicial combat by Thomas of Woodstock, Duke of Gloucester, uncle to Richard II, in Spelman, *Glossarium,* s.v. "Campus."

36. Du Cange, *Glossarium,* s.v. "Duellum."

37. Brussel (Nicolas), *Nouvel Examen de l'Usage Général des Fiefs en France* (Paris, 1727), 2:962.

38. *Ordonnances,* 1:16.

39. *Ordonnances,* 1:328, 390, 435.

40. Ferguson (Adam), *An Essay on the History of Civil Society* (Edinburgh, 1767), pt. 4, sec. 1.

II *The Command of the National Force*

1. Boulainvilliers (Henri, Count de), *Histoire de l'Ancien Gouvernment de la France* (The Hague, 1727), letter 12.

2. Velley (Paul François), *Histoire de France, depuis l'établissement de la monarchie jusqu'au règne de Louis XV* (Paris, 1763), 15:331, 389; 16:324.

3. Comines (Philippe de), *Mémoires,* Nouvelle édition, enrichie de notes et de figures, avec un recueil de traités par Messieurs Godefroy, augmentée par Lenglet du Fresnoy (Paris, 1747), 1:367.

4. Comines, *Mémoires,* 1:136.

5. Comines, *Mémoires,* 1:334. Charles VII levied taxes to the amount of 1,800,000 francs; Louis XI raised 4,700,000. The former had in pay 9,000 cavalry and 16,000 infantry. The latter augmented the cavalry to 15,000 and the infantry to 25,000. See Comines, *Mémoires,* 1:384. During the latter years of his reign he kept the greater part of these encamped in one place, and ready to march on the shortest warning (Ibid., p. 381).

6. Ibid., 1:358.

7. Ibid., bk. 5, chap. 15, pp. 309 ff.

Notes

8. Etudes de Mézeray (François), *Histoire de France depuis Faramond jusque au règne de Louis le Just* (Paris, 1685), 2:777.
9. Machiavelli, *Art of War*, bk. 2, chap. 2.
10. See Brantome (Pierre de Bourdeille), *Oeuvres* (The Hague, 1740), 10:18; and Fleuranges (Robert de la Marck), *Mémoires* (Paris, 1753), p. 143.
11. Comines, *Mémoires*, bk. 7, chap. 5, p. 440.
12. *Politica Imperialia*, ed. Melchoir Goldast (n.p., 1614), p. 980.

III The Political Constitution

1. Otto of Freising, *De Gestis Friderici Imperatoris*, bk. 2, chap. 20.
2. Otto of Freising, *De Gestis*, bk., 1, chap. 27; *Chronicon*, bk. 7, chaps. 27, 31; Muratori, *Annali d'Italia* (n.p., 1744), 9:398, 404.
3. Giovanni Villani, *Cronica*, bk. 12, chaps. 89 and 104; Vita di Cola di Rienzo," in Muratori, *Antiquitates*, 3:399 ff; Bénigne Dujardin Boispreaux, *Histoire de Nicolas Rienzy* (Paris, 1743), pp. 91 ff.
4. Sandi (Vettor), *Principi di Storia Civile della Repubblica di Venezia* (Venice, 1755), bk. 8, Chap. 16, pp. 891 ff.
5. Giannone (Pietro), *Istoria Civile del Regno di Napoli*, bk. 28, chap. 2, pp. 410 ff.
6. Ibid., p. 414.
7. Ibid., bk. 18, chap. 5; Burkhard Gotthelf Struve, *Corpus Historiae Germanicae* (Jena, 1730), 1:481.
8. Giannone, *Istoria Civile*, bk. 19, chap. 4, sec. 2.
9. Ibid., bk. 16, chap. 2.
10. Comines, *Mémoires*, 4, pt. 2:5.
11. Struve, *Corpus Historiae Germanicae*, 1:625.
12. Leibnitz (Gottfried Wilhelm von), *Codex Juris Gentium Diplomaticum* (Hannover, 1693), 1:257.
13. Ripalmonti (Giuseppe), *Urbis Mediolani Historiae Patriae Libri 10*, bk. 6, p. 654, in Struve, *Corpus Historiae Germanicae*, 1:930; Jean Dumont, *Corps Universel Diplomatique du Droit des Gens* (The Hague, 1726), 3, 2:333.
14. Assemanus (Josephus Simonius), *Italicae Historiae Scriptores* (Rome, 1751), 3:135.
15. Zurita (Geronimo), *Los Anales de la Corona de Aragon* (Saragossa, 1610), 4:113, 115.
16. See Ferreras (Juan de), *Histoire Général d'Espagne* (Paris, 1742), 7:92; Pierre-Joseph d'Orléans, *Histoire des Révolutions d'Espagne* (Paris, 1743), 3:155; and Lucius Marineus Siculus, *De Rebus Hispaniae Mirabilibus*, in Schott (Andreas), *Hispaniae Illustratae seu rerum urbiumque Hispaniae scriptores varii* (n.p., 1603), 1:429.
17. Mariana (Juan de), *Historiae de Rebus Hispaniae Libri 30*, bk. 23, chap. 9.
18. Martel (Geronimo), "Forma de Celebrar Cortes en Arragon," in Blancas (Gerònimo de), *Coronaziones de Los Serenissemos Reyes de Aragon* (Saragossa, 1641).
19. Ibid., p. 2.

20. Blancas (Geronimo), *Aragonensium rerum commentarii,* in Schott, *Hispaniae Illustratae . . . scriptores,* 3:750.

21. Martel, *Forma de Celebrar Cortes en Arragon,* p. 2.

22. Blancas, *Commentarii,* p. 763.

23. Blancas has preserved two responses of the Justiza to James II who reigned towards the close of the thirteenth century (*Commentarii,* p. 748).

24. Ibid., pp. 747–55.

25. Ibid., p. 720.

26. Ibid., p. 751.

27. Mariana, *Historiae. . . . Libri 30,* bk. 18, chap. 15.

28. Zurita, *Los Anales,* 6:22.

29. Mariana, *Historiae. . . . Libri 30,* bk. 25, chap. 5.

30. Zurita, *Los Anales,* 5:22; and Aelii Antonii Nebrissensis (Antonio de Lebrixa), *Rerum a Fernando et Elisàbe Hispaniarum Felicissimis Regibus Gestarum Decades Duae,* in Schott, *Hispaniae Illustratae Scriptores,* 1:860.

31. Montesquieu, *Esprit des Lois,* bk. 2, chap. 4; Ferguson, *An Essay on the History of Civil Society,* pt. 1, sec. 10.

32. Annalista Saxo, in Struve, *Corpus Historiae Germanicae,* 1:246.

33. Pfeffel, *Abrégé chronologique,* p. 120, 152.

34. Ibid., p. 154.

35. See Struve, *Corpus Historiae Germanicae,* 1:325.

36. Ibid., p. 510.

37. Pfeffel, *Abrégé chronologique,* p. 241.

38. Rycaut (Sir Paul), *The Present State of the Ottoman Empire* (London, 1668), p. 25.

39. Ibid., p. 8.

40. Demetrius (Kantemir), *The History of the Growth and Decay of the Ottoman Empire,* written originally in Latin (London, 1734), p. 87.

Index

Africa, 11
Alexander VI, Pope, 102, 125
Alfonso of Castile, 117
Alfonso of Naples, 108, 111
Alfred the Great, 21
America, 5, 13, 152, 153, 154
Ammianus Marcellinus, 150
Amurath, 146
Anderson, Adam, *An Historical and Chronological Deduction of the Origin of Commerce*, 173, 175, 176
Angouleme, Count of, 84
Anna Comnena, 24
Arabs, 61
Aragon, 109, 114, 116, 117, 118, 119, 121, 126, 172. *See also* Ferdinand, King of Aragon; Frederick of Aragon; John II of Aragon; Peter of Aragon
Aristotle, 172
Aurelian, 170
Austria, 90, 91, 137

Balance of power, 4, 17, 34, 71, 73, 87, 89, 139
Baluze, Stephan, editor of *Capitularia regum francorum*, 156, 166, 168, 169
Barbarians, barbarism, barbarous, 8, 10, 12, 13, 14, 15, 16, 19, 20, 22, 23, 25, 26, 27, 36, 38, 40, 45, 48, 51, 53, 54, 60, 62, 63, 68, 70, 97, 149, 151, 154, 155, 156, 161, 167, 168, 175
Beaumanoir, Philippe de Remi, *Coustumes de Beauvoisis*, 162, 168
Beehr, Matthias Joannes, *Rerum Mecleburgicarum libri octo*, 167, 169
Black Prince, 173
Blackstone, *Commentaries on the Laws of England*, 172
Boehmer, Georg Ludwig, *Principia juris feudalis*, 164
Bouquet, Martin, *Recueil des historiens des Gaules et de la France*, 160, 163, 165, 169, 170
Brussel, Nicolas, *Nouvel examen de l'usage général des fiefs*, 158, 160, 163, 168
Burgundy, 72, 83, 84, 85, 91. *See also* Charles the Bold; Mary of Burgundy

Caesar, 149, 150, 151, 152
Caliphs, 25, 114
Capet, Hugh, 128, 129
Capitularia. See Baluze
Castile, 114, 116, 117, 120, 121, 126. *See also* Alfonso of Castile; Henry IV of Castile; Isabella of Castile; John I of Castile

181

Index

Index

Socrates, 61

Solyman, 147, 148

Spain, 11, 31, 72, 82, 92, 95, 112, 113, 114, 115, 116, 122, 123, 124, 125, 127, 128, 171, 176. *See also* Aragon; Castile; Moors

Swiss, 80, 90, 91, 92, 112, 139

Tacitus, 149, 150, 151, 152, 157

Thales, 61

Theodosius, 13

Turks, 23, 25, 144, 145, 146, 147, 148. *See also* Amurath; Mahomet II; Solyman

Valentine Visconti, 111

Vandals, 8, 113, 114

Venice, Venetians, 25, 27, 28, 93, 94, 95, 98, 104, 105, 106, 107, 170, 173

Vic, Claude de, and Vaissete, Jean Joseph, *Histoire générale de Languedoc*, 158, 162

Visconti, 110. *See also* John Galeazzo Visconti; Philip Maria Visconti; Valentine Visconti

Wachter, Johann Georg, *Glossarium Germanicum*, 164

Westphalen, Ernst Joachim von, *Monumenta inedita rerum Germanicarum*, 168

William of Holland, German king, 137